The Story Behind Musical Instruments

The Story

Behind Musical Instruments

ELIZABETH RIDER MONTGOMERY

Illustrated by Mary Stevens

73914

DODD, MEAD & COMPANY · NEW YORK · 1961

Library of Congress Catalog Card Number: 53-9527

Printed in the United States of America

To Monty
whose instrument is the radio

Preface

Someone has said, "It takes three to make music: one to create, one to perform, and one to appreciate. And who can tell which is the most important?" *

For vocal music the statement is complete, but for instrumental music one factor is lacking. A fourth must be added: one to build the instrument.

It would be futile to speculate as to which of these four is the most important to music, but there is no doubt that the maker of instruments, like the other three, plays a vital role. Without instruments, no instrumental music could be performed or listened to, regardless of how much was created. A poor instrument is a stumbling-block to the finest artist, while a superb instrument is an inspiration.

Few musical instruments were really invented. Most of them just grew. Someone would improve one part of an instrument, a second man would improve something else, and still another would add a third refinement.

Seldom was an improvement in an instrument welcomed by contemporary musicians. Each new valve, each change in shape or bore, meant that a player must form new habits; sometimes it required learning to play all over again. Usually many years passed before an improvement was accepted as standard. By that time the details of its origin had been lost;

* Robert Haven Schauffler, from "The Creative Listener" in *Musical Amateur*.

occasionally even the name of the inventor was forgotten, or the honor ascribed to two or more entirely different men. The musical historian can find reams of material concerning composers and virtuosi, but pathetically little about the men who made the instruments which are a prime essential of their music.

Most of the stories in this book, therefore, are not actual history in the sense that documentary proof for the incidents can be furnished. . . . Perhaps it would be more accurate to say that while documentary proof for the material in this book *can* be furnished, one can find an equal amount of proof that the incidents happened at another place, or at another date, or to another man. The entire history of musical instruments seems full of contradictions.

Therefore, I have gathered as much evidence as I could find, both pro and con, on all matters concerned and have drawn my own conclusions. None of the incidents described is made up out of whole cloth; all are based on events and records which several reputable authorities consider authentic, but which some authorities reject. Conversation and thoughts ascribed to characters are, of course, imaginary.

Although I assume full responsibility for statements made in this book, I am indebted to many people for advice, criticism, and help in research. Chief of these are Francis Aranyi, director of the Youth Symphony Orchestra of the Pacific Northwest; Gordon Brown, director of band at West Seattle High School; Dr. Stanley Chapple, director of music at the University of Washington; Paul Giroux of the University of Washington; William F. Ludwig of the WFL Drum Company; Miss Marie Merrill, of the Seattle Public Library;

T. Stewart Smith, director of orchestra at West Seattle High School; George Lawrence Stone, president of N.A.R.D.; and Miss Jean Swanson of the music department of Mills College in Oakland, California.

The illustrations are intended to portray the pleasure people find in musical instruments rather than to serve as photographically accurate diagrams as to how to play these instruments.

E. R. M.

To the Reader

How would you like to work a jig-saw puzzle if, before you could put it together, you had to *find* all the pieces of the puzzle? And if you did not know how many pieces there were, or whether they were in your house or in your neighbor's . . . think what a job you would have!

Writing this STORY BEHIND MUSICAL INSTRUMENTS has been exactly that kind of a task: gathering up all the pieces of the puzzle and trying to fit them together, always wondering if there weren't some more parts somewhere.

Yet it has been fascinating work. I hope you will enjoy reading this story of the instruments that make our music as much as I enjoyed writing it.

E. R. M.

Contents

NOTE: The dates given are those of the particular incidents which are related.

PART ONE

Music from Strings

A STRADIVARIUS violin and a hunting bow.

You never thought of those together, did you? Yet they are definitely related. The hunting bow, without a doubt, was the original ancestor of the violin—of all stringed instruments, in fact.

Several thousand years ago Primitive Man, stalking game to feed his family, heard the musical twang of the bow-string as his arrow sped to its mark. Perhaps in gratitude or triumph he plucked the string again and again, enjoying the musical sound. Later on he tried to vary the tone, and he found that he could make it higher by pinching part of the string against the bow.

This unknown hunter had discovered two important principles about the production of music:

(1) *A string which is made to vibrate gives off a musical sound.*

(2) *The shorter the string, the higher the tone.*

Primitive Man didn't realize that the shorter string's higher pitch was due, not to its shortness, for that is only one of the factors that affect pitch, but to the faster vibrations caused by its shorter length. Now we know two more principles about the production of string music:

>   (3) *A rapidly vibrating string produces shorter sound-waves than a slowly vibrating one.*
>
>   (4) *The shorter the sound-wave, the higher the pitch.*

What the Pitch of a String Depends On

1. Length.

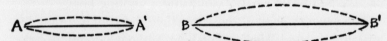

(A) is shorter. It vibrates through a smaller arc. Hence the vibrations are faster and the pitch is higher.

2. Thickness or weight.

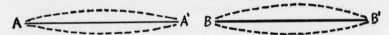

(A) is thinner and lighter. Hence it will vibrate faster and its pitch is higher.

3. Tension.

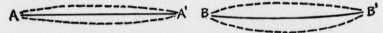

(A) is strung more tightly. Hence its vibrations will be shorter and faster and the pitch will be higher.

Heart of the Orchestra

Did you ever sing in a choir? Then you know how much bigger and richer is the music of a well-trained chorus than your voice alone can produce.

But even the biggest choir cannot compare with a symphony orchestra in range and variety of tone. The flutes and violins can sing higher than the highest soprano voice. The tubas and string basses can reach lower than the deepest bass voice. The oboes can wail more plaintively, the trombones can blare more loudly, the percussions more sharply, than any human voice. A modern symphony orchestra can reproduce almost any sound of nature or imagination.

The world has had musical instruments of one kind or another for several thousand years, but it has had orchestras for only about three hundred years. Although musicians had undoubtedly experimented from earliest times in trying different instruments together, until the seventeenth century instruments were used primarily to accompany vocal singing; and only the same or related instruments were used together.

The orchestra was born simultaneously with opera: a court musician of Florence, Italy, Jacopo Peri, wrote an opera, *Euridice,* to celebrate the royal marriage of Maria d'Medici in March, 1600, and as accompaniment he used a mixed group of instruments which was the ancestor of our symphony orchestra.

The long delay in the birth of the orchestra was due partly

to the fact that practically no music was written for instruments—only for voices—and partly because instruments were so imperfect that their tones were too inaccurate for ensemble playing. As instruments improved, more music was written for them, and as more music was written, instruments were improved in order to be able to play it. So the symphony orchestra grew in quality and ability until it became the versatile and superb thing it is today.

1. Spirit of the Renaissance

Can you imagine a stew without meat? Or a home without a kitchen?

An orchestra without violins would be as uncharacteristic as a meat-less stew or a kitchen-less house. It simply would not be an orchestra.

The very first orchestras were composed largely of violins and brothers of this instrument, plus the harpsichord. Even today, more than half of the symphony orchestra is made up of stringed instruments, and two thirds of those are violins. It is no accident that the concertmaster (the person next in authority to the conductor himself) is the leader of the first violins—the leader of the main group of the biggest family in the orchestra: before the days of the baton-wielding conductor, the solo violinist led his fellow-musicians, and was actually responsible for the entire performance.

Like all stringed instruments, the violin family descended from the hunting bow. Although we know that the earliest instrument had only one string, we cannot trace the steps of the violin's descent. No one knows for sure which of the many stringed instruments of the Middle Ages (harp, lute, lyre, rebec, crwth, viol, etc.) was the immediate ancestor of our violin. No one is positive who made the first one; in fact, there is great disagreement on that point. Some seem to think the honor should go to Gasparo da Salo of Brescia, Italy, and some favor Andrea Amati, who worked at Cremona at the same time. Others feel that the bulk of the evidence seems to indicate that the first violin-maker was a German who moved to France. If so, it may have come about something like this.

At the beginning of the sixteenth century, Gaspard Duiffoprugcar had been for years a successful mosaic worker and luthier (or instrument maker, particularly of lutes) in Bologna, in partnership with his brother Uldrich. About 1516, when the King of France, Francis I, went to Bologna to sign a treaty with Pope Leo X, he heard of Gaspard's work and asked him to become instrument maker for his Royal Chapel in Paris.

Naturally this royal recognition flattered Gaspard Duiffoprugcar. But it was not without some qualms that he left his prosperous business to his brother's care and journeyed to

Paris. Royal patrons, he knew, could be hard to please. Royal favor did not always last, especially if the jealousy of some court favorite was aroused.

But it was Gaspard himself who first became dissatisfied with the arrangement. Paris did not agree with him. (Whether it was the climate, or whether the petty jealousies and intrigues of court life were too much for him, we do not know.) At any rate, Gaspard left Paris to stay with the Cardinal of Ferrara near Lyons, about two hundred miles away. There he carried on his work for the court musicians and was content.

It was a great time to be alive. Europe was awakening, after the period we call the Dark Ages, to the possibilities of culture, of science and literature, of art and music. Progressive thinkers and great artists had appeared on the scene, especially in Italy: Leonardo da Vinci, Benvenuto Cellini, Christopher Columbus, Raphael, Michelangelo, and many others. Gaspard Duiffoprugcar had heard much of their work, and had seen enough samples to be convinced of their genius. He had even met Da Vinci at the Court of France and talked to him. An astounding man! His genius reached in so many directions.

Yes, beauty was in the air in the sixteenth century. Gaspard saw it in the Gothic architecture of the buildings about him, and in the paintings of the fast-growing school of artists. He heard it in the choral music of the churches and in the strains of lyre and lute, of psaltery and dulcimer and rebab, of harp and viol.

Especially the viol. Of all the instruments he made or repaired, Gaspard loved the viol family. It had come to be the most important group of instruments, the most in demand at royal functions and large gatherings. And rightly so. For was not the viol the most advanced of all instruments in style and shape? With incurved sides, fretted finger-board, a bridge under its six strings, it produced a sweet and plaintive tone when the bow, held palm up, was drawn across its strings. No other instrument could boast such a pleasing sustained tone as the viols, from the large viola da gamba (held between the legs) to the small viola da braccio (held on the arm or rested against the knee). The new instrument maker for the Royal Court of France felt that the viol family, in all its forms, was destined to be the musical leader of the world. He determined to make viols as fine as any that had ever been made.

But the atmosphere of the time was not filled with beauty alone; progress was the keynote. It was not enough, in those inspiring days of the Renaissance, to make buildings or paintings or instruments in the customary fashion, no matter how beautiful the workmanship. One must progress, improve, innovate. Strive for something new, something better.

So Gaspard Duiffoprugcar, in keeping with the spirit of his time, set himself not only to make beautiful viols, but to create a new form of the instrument. He tried many variations: flatter back and rounder back; shorter, tighter strings and longer, looser strings; more strings and fewer strings; square shoulders and more sloping shoulders. He adapted to the viol features of several other instruments: the peg-box of the guitar, the rounded bridge of the rubebe, the f-shaped holes of the vielle instead of the viol's customary c-shaped holes.

And always Gaspard added the beautiful inlay or mosaic

work for which he was famous. (On the back of a bass viol still in existence, for example, he inlaid with different-colored woods a map of the city of Paris.)

Some of his variations from the traditional viol shape were such obvious failures that he did not try them again. Others, which seemed to improve the tone or the ease of playing, he used over and over.

Eventually Gaspard made for King Francis a group of instruments which embodied his progressive ideas. These, though heavy and clumsy by modern standards (far from being true violins as we know the instrument today), were perhaps the first instruments to show the beginnings of violin characteristics: rounded backs, square shoulders, well-defined curves and corners, only four strings—shorter and heavier and more taut than the viol's—and no frets on the fingerboards. The backs of his instruments were laboriously and beautifully inlaid, and their tone was powerful and penetrating beyond anything that had ever been dreamed possible —although today we would call it weak.

Doubtless Gaspard Duiffoprugcar never knew (if he was indeed the man who originated the true violin form) that he had done anything more than make a slightly original type of viol. He did not realize that, in taking the first step away from the traditional form, he was blazing the trail for the development of a new and better instrument that would be worthy to stand beside the paintings of Raphael and Da Vinci, the discoveries of Columbus, the silver masterpieces of Cellini, and all the other marvels that came out of that incredible age of progress, the Renaissance.

2. Founder of a School

The man who first had the courage and imagination to depart from the traditional style of viol-making performed a great service for music. However, there is no doubt that the earliest of these new instruments were as primitive in comparison with a fine Stradivarius or Guarnerius as a 1912 Ford is beside today's streamlined model. The violin had begun to evolve, but it had a long, long way to go.

We will probably never know whether Gaspard Duiffoprugcar or Gasparo da Salo or some other was the originator of the violin form; but we do know who it was that took the germ of this idea and developed a system which made possible the ultimate perfection of the new instrument in less than a century—the most rapid progress made by any major instrument.

By the middle of the sixteenth century, Southern Europe had begun to be conscious of the little town of Cremona, on the banks of the Po River. From the fall of the Roman Empire, the town had been a battle-ground. But wars were only unpleasant interludes in the business of living; after every siege its citizens had resumed their quiet life and work.

The show place of Cremona was its stately Cathedral. To the townspeople the Cathedral was not only a thing of beauty; it was an inspiration—in a religious sense, naturally, and in music and art as well. The Cathedral's demand for beautiful frescos and inspiring murals stimulated the growth of a school of painting, and the monks' interest in music encouraged many residents of Cremona to take up the study of music.

Naturally, as the number and quality of musicians increased, the demand for more and better instruments rose also. By 1550 Cremona had gained a reputation as a center of instrument making that rivaled that of Brescia, forty miles away, which had long been considered the leader in that field.

The man who was principally responsible for the growing renown of Cremona was Andrea Amati, whose family had been respected citizens of Cremona for over five hundred years.

Andrea's little workshop faced the west front of San Domenico Church. How he happened to take up the profession of luthier (instrument maker) we do not know, or where he learned his trade, or when or where he first saw one of the revolutionary square-shouldered viols. Some authorities believe that the Duiffoprugcar instruments are not genuine, and that Andrea Amati was the one who evolved the violin from the viol. At any rate, it is certain that by the middle of the sixteenth century Amati was making real violins, and violins which were far superior to those of his contemporary, Gasparo da Salo of Brescia.

Like all instrument makers of the time, Amati made any and all instruments that were in demand. Although the new-fangled violin was becoming popular, it had by no means displaced the old viols, and Amati had many calls for viols of various sizes, as well as rebecs and lutes.

But the violin was his real love. Patiently, tirelessly, he worked to improve it, always seeking sweetness of tone rather than power. The symphony orchestra and the big concert hall were unknown at that time; music belonged in the palaces of kings and dukes, except for the organs and trombones of the churches and the trumpets and drums of the town bands. Such ensemble music as was played in those days was under the sponsorship of royalty, in relatively small rooms, and power of tone was neither needed nor wanted.

By the time Andrea's sons, Antonio and Geronimo, were old enough to be of much help to him in his workshop, he had made of the crude and clumsy violin a small and delicate instrument, characterized by higher arching of the back and belly and by a sweet, tender, mellow tone.

Amati had taken his sons into his shop as soon as they were big enough to hold a glue pot. His younger brother Nicolo, who had finished his apprenticeship, often helped him, too. Andrea Amati encouraged them all to watch and listen and help.

"I learn new things every day," Amati would say to the two little boys and the older boy as he carefully tested a tuning peg for size before resuming his whittling. "Better ways of joining . . . finer varnish . . . better proportions . . . which woods make the sweetest tone. What I learn must not be forgotten. You boys must remember it all—every bit of what I have discovered about violin-making. After I am gone, you, too, will go on learning and will add to the store of skill and knowledge. You will teach your sons, and they in turn will continue to build on what you have given them, and add their own contributions. Only thus can the craft of violin-making grow and prosper until perfect instruments can be made."

Three heads nodded solemnly. Six attentive eyes watched Andrea Amati's skilful hands push the perfectly fitting peg into its hole.

Years later, in the 1570's, Amati's brother and sons had reason to be very glad they had watched and listened so carefully to everything the master-craftsman could teach them.

A messenger came from the king of France, Charles IX. Amati received him with the deference due an emissary of such an exalted personage.

The messenger introduced himself as Monsieur Nicolas Delinet, a member of the King's Band. "His Majesty, King Charles, wishes you to make some instruments for use in the

Royal Chapel."

Amati bowed. "I will be very happy to construct any instruments His Majesty wishes."

"All of them are to be of the new viol shape. Twenty-four of the ones called violins, twelve large and twelve small; six violas; and eight basses. He wishes all of them constructed of the very best wood. . . ." And Delinet went on to give particulars of the royal order.

Nicolo Amati and the two boys had been listening, open-mouthed, in the background. This was far the largest and most important order that had ever come to the unpretentious shop.

When the messenger had gone, Andrea turned to them, excited, pleased, and more than a trifle apprehensive. "You heard? A huge order! And for the King of France! What recompense it promises, both in money and prestige. But . . . I wonder . . . will I be able to execute this commission satisfactorily?"

The boys crowded around him, reassuring him loyally. Of course, he would! No one could make as fine instruments as he. If it were not so, and if it were not well known, would the King of France have sent to him for his instruments?

Amati smiled. Nevertheless, he did not underestimate the magnitude of building thirty-eight instruments in the time allotted. And he would rather lose a sale—even so big and important a sale as this—than let a single instrument go out from his shop unless it was as perfect as human hands could make it.

However, he would not have to work alone. He looked around him at the eager faces of his brother Nicolo and his sons, Antonio and Geronimo. All three were now excellent craftsmen; he had even taken Nicolo into partnership. Andrea himself would oversee all of the work on this royal order, and he would do all the actual building and finishing, but much of the preparatory work could be performed by these others.

Many months—perhaps years—later, the last instrument of the French king's order was finished. Andrea and his helpers gazed at the array with justifiable pride. The workmanship was beautiful; they could say it honestly, knowing the loving care that had gone into the fitting and finishing of every single part. The golden amber varnish was the best they had made yet. And on the back of each instrument was painted the arms of France and the avowed motto of Charles IX, *Pietate et Justita*. Yes, truly this lot of nearly forty instruments was a worthy representation of the skill of the Amati family of Cremona.

Andrea was proud and happy, not so much because of his own work as of the growing skill of his brother and his sons. They were proving apt and devoted disciples. They would carry on his trade and his name. They would be true to his ideals of fine craftsmanship and continued progress. He had founded something that would live.

And so he had. Andrea Amati's sons carried on his name and his business. Although they did not add much in the way of originality and progress, they transmitted faithfully to their sons the heritage of skill and knowledge their father had given to them. Geronimo's son, Nicolo the second, became the greatest violin-maker of the name of Amati—the greatest instrument maker the little town of Cremona had known up to that time.

But why shouldn't the grandson of Andrea Amati be great? Did he not have bequeathed to him the sum of all that his father and his grandfather had learned of the fine art of violin-making?

3. Learn the Rules—Then Test Them

Can you imagine quadruplets, born at the same time, yet of vastly different sizes and voices?

Of the four families of instruments that make up the modern symphony orchestra (strings, woodwinds, brasses, and percussion), only the strings, or violin family, are such a close-knit unit that they resemble quadruplets. The small, fragile-looking violin, with a power of tone out of all proportion to its size; the slightly larger viola, with its deeper, more plaintive voice; the masterful cello, with its rich tenor voice; and the huge double-bass, with its slow, booming notes—all these are so similar in construction, so nearly identical in growth, that the history of one is the history of all. The great violin makers produced all members of the violin family. Some excelled in cellos or basses; some in violins. But by and large a master of the craft made of practically every instrument he undertook a masterpiece.

There are many famous names in the roster of violin makers. Stradivarius, Guarnerius, Stainer, Amati—these are names everyone recognizes. While Stradivarius is acknowledged to be the greatest violin maker who ever lived, the Amatis were the greatest *family* of violin makers. However, they are remembered today not so much because of the school of violin-making which Andrea, the first Amati, founded; they are remembered and revered because of a product of that school: its most famous pupil.

By the time Nicolo the Second, grandson of Andrea, was an old man, Cremona had become widely known as the home of fine violins, violas and cellos. The craft of violin-making had spread over the town until the stringed instrument—particularly the violin—dominated the life of its citizens.

The average Cremona boy dreamed of becoming a great violin-maker, as the normal boy of Oberammergau dreams of playing a part in the Passion Play. While he was very young, a boy was apprenticed to the best master available. Nicolo Amati would be his choice, undoubtedly, but a master could take only a limited number of students.

For years the apprentice would perform the most menial

and uninteresting tasks: sweep out the shop, keep up the fires, clear the work benches. But all the time he would watch and listen and learn. Gradually he would be advanced to chores closer to the coveted task of instrument-making: he would sharpen tools, prepare glue, perhaps even cut down a tree his master had selected as good violin material, and saw it on the quarter.

After months—or years—he was allowed to mix varnish, to help with the glueing, and even to block out a model, or use one of the tiny planes in the early stages of planing. When he had proved himself adept at every phase of the work, he was permitted to make a violin by himself from start to finish. Eventually the great day arrived when his master inspected his work, pronounced it good, and told him to sign his name. His dream had come true: after long years of apprenticeship he was a violin-maker at last!

But the dream had not really come true yet, after all, for if the apprentice was a typical Cremona boy, he had dreamed of being a "great" violin-maker. And greatness does not descend full-blown upon one. No matter how inspiring a teacher is, no matter how outstanding the capabilities of the student, only maturity and years of experience can bring those abilities to full fruit so the world will call him great.

And so it was with Stradivarius, the apprentice of Nicolo Amati. This man was the greatest violin-maker who ever lived, but he did not become great all at once. Strangely, very little is actually known about him, except what can be deduced from the marvelous instruments he left. Perhaps he reached the pinnacle of his career something like this.

Very early one morning in 1684, Antonius Stradivarius, son of a Cremona cloth merchant, was busy as usual in his workshop on the top floor of No. 2 Piazza San Domenico. His tall thin figure, encased in a white leather apron, with a white cap on his head, bent over his work bench. His strong, varnish-stained hands moved gently and skilfully as he adjusted the bridge and the strings of a finished instrument.

Forty years old, Stradivarius thought. For nearly thirty of those years he had lived with and for violin-making; at the age of thirteen he had made his first violin. Almost twenty years, now, since he had finished his apprenticeship with Nicolo Amati and started in business for himself, around the corner from Amati's shop. Now he was well established. By working early and late, he managed to make a good living for his growing family. His craftsmanship had gained a solid reputation. The name of Stradivarius was known fully as widely as that of his former fellow-apprentice, Andrea Guarnerius, whose workshop was only a few doors away.

As was the custom of violin makers, Stradivarius placed his label (made with a wood block) inside the newly finished instrument. He turned the violin lovingly in his hands and inspected it carefully. Then he took up the bow, tightened its strand of hair by slipping its loop to another notch on the ratchet device at the frog. Tucking the instrument under his chin, he played snatches of melodies to test the tone. . . . Not bad. Of course, the tone would be richer later on when the varnish and the wood had had time to fuse. And in the hands of an expert musician the violin would yield far sweeter music; he himself made no pretence of being a virtuoso, but he could play well enough to be certain when he had made a good instrument.

And this one was good—as fine a violin as could be purchased anywhere.

Nevertheless, Stradivarius frowned, dissatisfied, as he laid the instrument down and put away his planes and knives. It was a fine violin, yes. But it might almost have been made by his dear old teacher, Nicolo Amati. Except for trifling changes in the scroll, for these twenty years he had followed almost slavishly the precepts he had learned as an apprentice. Good? Of course, they were good precepts; Nicolo had been a truly great craftsman, the best of three generations of fine artisans. But he did not have the last word on violin-making; he admitted it himself.

"I am indebted to my father and his father for much of my success," he had told his devoted apprentices. "I could not have advanced the art of violin-making nearly as much as I have if I had not had their experience to build on. Now you boys have an even greater backlog to start with. Who knows to what heights the art can attain in your generation?"

Old Nicolo was gone now. His tools, which he had bequeathed to Stradivarius, were here in this very shop, used lovingly and reverently every day.

Stradivarius looked again at his newly completed instrument. So far he had merely mastered the craft that Nicolo had handed down to him; he had added nothing new. If he should die tomorrow, he would be remembered only by his family and his friends. If any of his violins were cherished, it would be because they were so much like Nicolo's. Surely, now that he knew the rules of his craft, it was time to test them to find out for himself whether they admitted of improvement.

Through the following months, Stradivarius followed his usual routine. He reached his shop early in the morning before his apprentices were awake; he worked long after he let them quit for the day. He supervised and taught his apprentices, including his eldest son Francesco. He answered the endless questions of his little son, Omobino. He filled his orders with meticulously made instruments of Nicolo Amati's style. He studied each violin of other makers that came to his hand, particularly a large Maggini, and all the time he was thinking, wondering, and feeling.

What should a perfect violin have? Sweet tone, of course. And Nicolo's instruments had that. But shouldn't it have power, too? The churches were asking constantly for stronger-toned instruments to assist the choral singing. And this new music-drama form he had heard about, called "opera"; powerful tone would certainly be welcome there. As long as music had been confined to smaller rooms in private houses or palaces, the sweet delicate music of the Amati-type violin sufficed. Now that big church sanctuaries and immense halls were coming into use, more volume was required from instruments.

Powerful tone . . . plus sweetness. That was what Stradivarius would work for.

Now, which ingredients of the Amati model were most responsible for its sweetness of tone? The choice of wood? Certainly the acoustical properties of the wood had a tremendous bearing on tone. . . . The high-arched belly? The importance of the size and shape of the sound-box could not be denied; the vibrations of the strings must be amplified. . . . The position of the sound-bar? An essential factor, without a doubt; the sound-bar must be perfectly placed so as to transmit to the sound-box the vibrations of the strings. . . . Well, he would find out which of these things were the most important.

For years Stradivarius experimented, methodically and painstakingly. Hardwood, soft wood, or some of each. Different thicknesses of wood for different parts. Lower arch, different-curved arch. The back of one piece, or of two pieces. Thicker sound-bar and thinner one. Different positions for the sound-bar; an eighth of an inch one way, an eighth of an inch the other. Ribs, lining, blocks, bridge, pegs, strings, varnish—every single detail of his craft came in for its share of experiment and testing—even instrument cases. He made numerous sketches and notes, accumulated favorite planks which had proved to have excellent acoustical properties, and perfected a recipe for slow-drying oil varnish which he wrote on the fly-leaf of the family Bible.

Although he made comparatively few violins during these years of experiment and research, Stradivarius filled at least one large order for the Prince of Tuscany, comprising several violins, violas and cellos. The cases were suitably decorated as befitted royal instruments. The order was delivered to the Prince in 1690.

That same year Stradivarius brought out his famous "Long Strad." To the world, which did not know of the long years of experimentation, the appearance of this innovation seemed abrupt, unaccountable. But it was undoubtedly a logical result of his scientific research.

Now that he had learned at first hand the secrets of resonance, purity of tone, and intensity, Stradivarius was trying out one of several possible combinations of the essential factors. The next few years saw him trying other combinations, retaining the width of the "Long Strad" but shortening the length, and so on. The master craftsman had become a creative artist.

By the end of that decade—and the century—Stradivarius had settled once and for all in his own mind the major questions of violin construction. He was to keep on working for thirty-five years longer (until he was past ninety) and would make, including other instruments besides violins, a total of well over a thousand instruments—no two exactly alike. But he never varied thereafter in the fundamental points that affected quality and intensity of tone.

The violins that came from the hand of Antonius Stradivarius in his golden years of 1700 to 1725 were marvels of grandeur and symmetry. He had improved the Amati violin in four main ways: (1) lowered the height of the belly, making the arch more uniform, to secure greater resistance to the pressure of the strings; (2) strengthened the corner blocks, for the same reason; (3) changed the setting of the sound-holes, to secure greater sonority; and (4) increased the size and strength of the scroll to resist splitting and to make a better balanced instrument in the hands of the player. The result was a violin of sweet, pure tone combined with greatly increased volume—an instrument that satisfied perfectly the demands of opera and the young symphony orchestra.

By the time Stradivarius laid down his tools at the age of ninety-odd, his fame had reached the length and breadth of Europe. A list of his customers, if he had bothered to keep one, would have read like a roster of royalty and nobility of half of Europe: King Charles III of Spain, the Elector of Poland, the Prince of Tuscany, the Duke of Alba, Cardinal Orsini, the Duke of Medina, and so on. Even King James II of England had received a complete set of instruments from his hand. Only in France and Germany the instruments of Stradivarius were little known until much later. Viotti, the founder of modern violin playing, brought the work of Stradivarius to the attention of the French near the end of the eighteenth century.

Thus in a long lifetime consecrated to a single ideal, Antonius Stradivarius brought the violin so near perfection that his work has never been surpassed. Improvements which have been made since are so minor that today, two and a half centuries later, a genuine Stradivarius violin remains the acme of quality. Instruments which sold during his lifetime for four gold louis (or about twenty dollars) are worth a fortune today.

4. Stradivarius of the Bow

Did you ever try to play a violin with an ordinary stick in place of a bow? Or did you ever, after playing with an ordinary cheap bow, suddenly switch to a fine, expensive one? Then you know how much depends on the bow in violin playing. It is to the violinist what breathing is to the singer. As one teacher puts it, "In the bow is the music."

The chief defect of early stringed instruments was the impossibility of sustained tones. The notes of wind instruments could be prolonged, but once a string was struck or plucked, the tone was there for an instant only.

Eventually some unknown genius discovered that rubbing a string with hair produced a steady continuous tone which could be made louder or softer according to the pressure.

Stradivarius perfected the violin. Soon after the year 1700 the violin, alone of all our modern instruments except the trombone, had reached the form it has today. But the violin bow was another matter. For many years after Stradivarius died, violinists used a crude bow utterly out of keeping with the perfection of their instruments. Made of reed, or some light wood, the bow was perfectly straight, or even curved outward somewhat like the hunting bow from which it had evolved. A cluster of coarse hair was fastened permanently at the tip; it could be tightened at the other end by slipping the loop from notch to notch of a small ratchet which was attached to the side of the stick. It is difficult to understand how a violinist could have produced music with such a bow. Yet Corelli, Tartini, and Vivaldi, contemporaries of Stradivarius, knew nothing better.

Although Stradivarius made bows as well as instruments of all sorts, he never turned his inventive powers toward the improvement of the bow. It was left for a boy who was born ten years after the master violin craftsman died to undertake the work that was to earn for him the title, "Stradivarius of the bow."

In 1775 the Tourte's of Paris, father and son Xavier, were known all over France as excellent bow-makers. The younger son, Francois, had been apprenticed to a watchmaker when he was very small, but he had not liked the trade. At the end of his eight-year apprenticeship he returned to his father's shop and took up the more interesting craft of bow-making, determined to win a place for himself in the family firm.

The elder Tourte had devised a nut that screwed into the bow stick to replace the ratchet device for tightening the hair, although the hair was still fastened in a round strand. This one improvement alone made Tourte violin bows sought after, and spread the fame of Tourte abroad.

But the Tourtes, father and Xavier and Francois, were still dissatisfied with their product. They held long and earnest discussions on the subject.

"Strong the bow must be, that is certain," Tourte, senior, affirmed.

"And flexible," added Xavier, the elder son.

"Strong and flexible, but not heavy," Francois summed it up. "That is what violinists are always asking for. The bow must not tire the hand, yet it must be capable of pressure."

The others nodded. "Yes, but how can one achieve strength without weight? It doesn't seem possible."

Francois leaned forward eagerly. "There is only one way to find out. We must experiment. Try out many kinds of wood, many lengths and shapes of bow."

"Experimenting takes time and materials. We have work to do, orders to fill."

"Please, Father. Please let me see what I can discover."

The elder Tourte was quite willing for Francois the novice to experiment, but he was reluctant to allow good materials to be wasted. So Francois used scraps and cast-off materials at first.

His early experiments were disappointing. Regardless of the wood he used, if he made the bow strong enough, it was too heavy. If he made it light in weight, it snapped in two. He seemed to make no progress at all.

But yes, he had made progress: he had determined that none of the woods they had been using was suitable for the kind of bow they wanted to make. He must look outside the shop to find new materials.

So the youngest of the Tourtes took long walks out of Paris, looking for different wood to try. Sometimes he came back with three or four branches or boards; often he returned empty-handed. On Sundays and long evenings; as he pursued his favorite sport of fishing in the Seine, he mulled over the knotty problem of obtaining strength without weight. But he could arrive at no solution, nor could he find any wood that answered his purpose.

One day Francois stood at the window of the shop on the fourth floor of No. 10 Quai d'Ecolo. His thoughts were busy with the paradox of lightness and strength, while his eyes roamed idly over the courtyard below.

"I wonder what kind of wood is used in barrel staves," he thought as his eyes came to rest on some empty sugar casks. "The wood must be flexible, for the staves are bent. I wonder if it is strong. . . ."

On an impulse he ran down the three flights of stairs and ripped several staves from a barrel.

Up in the workshop once more, Francois examined the wood. He had no idea what tree it came from; he had never seen this grain before. Fine but strong texture; perfectly straight grain. Well, it would do no harm to try. He began to cut a slender bow stick from one of the barrel staves.

Shaped and smoothed at last, fitted with a nut and mounted with hair, the bow was a disappointment. It could stand no more tension than other bows he had made.

Francois started to throw down the snapped bow in disdain. Then he paused and looked from it to the unused barrel staves. A revolutionary idea came into his head.

Suppose he bent the bow stick the other way? Suppose, instead of making it curve out, he made it *curve in* toward the hair? Could he, perhaps, in that way achieve greater strength while retaining the lightness of this unknown wood?

His radical plan was not as easy to carry out as it first appeared. He could bend the wood, but making it retain its curve was quite another matter. After many experiments, however, he found that he could give a bow any permanent curve he wished by subjecting it, properly shaped, to a certain degree of heat for a considerable time. And when his new bow was complete with fittings he was delighted to discover that it was both light and strong. He was on the right track.

The Tourte firm was jubilant. Now they could make bows which would be in demand all over the world. Xavier set himself to designing beautiful fittings worthy of such a bow.

But Francois was not ready by any means to have his new-type bow made in numbers. He had only begun his work. By now he realized that bow-making should be a science as exact as that of violin-making. How long should the bow be? How much of a curve should it have? How far from the stick should the hair be? What kind of hair should be used, and how much? There was absolutely no uniformity in bows of the period, no rules whatever. Each violinist and each maker had his own preferences. Francois Tourte knew that he must study intensively the science of bow-making and learn more —much more—before he could say that he knew exactly how a violin bow should be made.

Soon after that, one of the finest violinists of the day, Giovanni Battista Viotti, an Italian who had studied under Pugnani, came to Paris for a series of concerts. Naturally, he gravitated to the bow-making shop of the Tourtes. When he saw the revolutionary new bow of Francois, he was at first astounded and then—as he tried it—delighted.

"Marvelous! Marvelous!" cried Viotti. "Why, I can play almost to the tip. Even tone all the way. And *such* tone! I did not know this Stradivarius of mine had such music in it."

Xavier and his father nodded proudly. Had they not said this bow was the best ever made?

But Francois, instead of bowing and smiling, was asking questions. "Does it seem light to your hand?"

Viotti considered. "Lighter, by far, than my old one. But still not balanced. Balance is very important."

"Would it be better if it were longer? Or if the stick were tapered toward the tip?"

That was the beginning of an odd but satisfying partnership. Francois made many experimental bows: longer, shorter; same thickness throughout, tapered; greater curve, less curve; more hairs, fewer; and so on. Viotti, who came often to the shop, tested each bow, quick to note whether a change was an improvement or a retrogression, constantly suggesting other possibilities.

Francois kept careful track of all his experiments and their results. And always he continued the search for the perfect wood. The barrel staves, he had long since learned, came from Brazil and were probably pernambuco wood. He ordered some of this wood from Brazil, and it proved to be, indeed, ideal for his purpose.

Several difficulties stood in the way, however, of getting an adequate supply of pernambuco wood to make his bows in quantity. Most of this wood was knotty and crooked, and he had to have straight grain for violin bows. Sometimes in eight or ten tons he would find only one or two pieces suitable for his use.

As if that was not enough to try his patience and his pocketbook, shipping became uncertain and expensive because of the American War for Independence and the resumption of hostilities between France and England. The price of pernambuco wood rose to nearly five shillings a pound.

But Francois Tourte persevered. Neither the price of the wood nor the difficulty of getting it would keep him from using the best possible material for his violin bows, once he had determined on the best. By his long and careful experimentation and research, aided by Viotti's advice, he ascertained the perfect proportions of the bow, the best possible curve for the stick, the ideal degree of tapering, and the proper distance of the hair from the stick.

He gave a great deal of study to the hair itself, trying hair from different animals. He found that white hair from the tail of certain male horses gave the best results. The hairs had to be carefully selected; only long, well-rounded ones would do. Half of them must be set in with the roots at the frog and half with the roots at the tip, to obtain friction from the bow on both up-bow and down-bow. (We know now that this is because horse hairs are covered with a layer of over-lapping scales which offer resistance to the strings and produce the necessary friction.)

Finally, at Viotti's request for something to prevent the hair from twisting, Francois invented a metal band to spread the hairs smoothly before they entered the nut, instead of leaving them in a round bunch.

The violin bow was at last perfected. When the wars were over the Tourtes could make them in quantity, but all his life Francois insisted on destroying all bows which were not up to his standard of excellence.

Viotti, of course, was the first to use the Tourte bow in concert. His "sweep of the whole bow," which had been impossible up to then, amazed his audience. In fact, the technique of modern violin-playing really began with Viotti, who played on a Stradivarius instrument with a bow made by Francois Tourte, the Stradivarius of the bow.

Free-Lance Strings

Of all the many stringed instruments of history, only the violin and its brothers are regular members of the modern symphony orchestra. But numerous other stringed instruments are used and loved all over the world.

Practically every country, every people, has its favorite instrument. In Southern Europe it is the mandoline, which is a kind of alto lute. Played with a pick or plectrum, its strings are tuned in pairs. This little instrument is very popular for accompaniment to singing. Whole orchestras are sometimes formed of mandolines of different sizes.

Our own Southern States favor the banjo. This long-necked instrument, with a drumhead stretched over a wooden resonator, is believed to have evolved from a primitive African instrument, with one or two strings, known as the banjar.

The national instrument of Spain is the guitar, a descendant of the ancient cither. It is played like the lute, by plucking the strings with the fingers or a plectrum. The guitar is so widely used in Spain that it takes the place of the piano in that country.

The Hawaiian or steel guitar is merely the ordinary guitar strung with steel strings in place of gut, and with a special bridge. It is played with a plectrum and a steel pressure bar for the strings.

All of these instruments, while used in the symphony orchestra only for special effects, are widely used in dance bands and for folk music. Each has its special quality of music and its own individual appeal.

5. From an Inquisitive Mind

Of all the free-lance strings, the concert harp occupies a special place. It is a more or less regular member of the orchestra, yet it holds aloof. It does not consider itself a member of the string section, still less of the woodwinds, brasses, or percussion. The harp stands alone—literally—even in its position on the stage in a concert.

A lineal descendant of the hunting bow, the harp is more than five thousand years old. It is one of the most ancient, the most honored, and the most widespread of instruments. It was known in early Bible times, and long before that in various Asiatic countries. Practically every race has used some form of harp. In ancient Wales it was considered a royal instrument; slaves were forbidden to touch it, on pain of death. Even today the harp is the national instrument of Ireland, possibly the only musical instrument adopted as a national symbol.

In spite of the harp's great antiquity, the concert harp is a relatively young instrument. Until the sixteenth century a player could change the pitch of a string only by pressing it with his finger. And it was less than a hundred and fifty years ago that the harp became an adaptable instrument, playable in any key.

In 1768 sixteen-year-old Sebastien Erard of Strassburg went to Paris to seek his fortune.

He had studied architecture and drawing and geometry, but had always spent his happiest hours helping his father, a cabinet-maker. Now his father was dead. As the eldest son, Sebastien felt responsible for the security of his family. Paris offered a wider field for his talents than Strassburg, so to Paris he went.

It was not hard for a strong, enterprising boy to get a job. Sebastien soon found work in the shop of a harpsichord maker. Shortly he became an excellent craftsman because of his clever hands and his powers of observation. But his insatiable curiosity and independent thinking got him into trouble; his employer expected blind obedience, not intelligent initiative, and Sebastien was discharged.

The boy's second employer, another harpsichord maker, was more appreciative of his talents. He encouraged Sebastien to learn every phase of the business, including why and how instruments worked. Before long young Erard became known as the cleverest workman in the shop.

His reputation for ingenuity spread. Other instrument makers heard about him. When one of them received a special order which he did not know how to execute, he called on Sebastien Erard for help. The boy figured out how to make the desired instrument and built it.

Later on Sebastien invented a mechanical harpsichord for the cabinet of curiosities of Monsieur de la Blauchire. This novelty created a sensation in the musical world of Paris and focused attention on young Erard. He became acquainted with many influential people.

Naturally the twenty-year-old boy found this success extremely pleasant. Even more pleasant was something unexpected which resulted from his sudden fame. One of his new acquaintances invited him to accompany him to the chateau of the Duchess of Villeroi, a wealthy patroness of the arts who was especially interested in music.

The young workman tried not to be overwhelmed by the luxury he found in the villa and the wealth and power represented by the great lady to whom he was introduced.

"I have been hearing on all sides of the genius of Monsieur Erard," the Duchess told him. "And now I find you are as personable as you are clever."

Sebastien acknowledged the compliment courteously.

"I want you to come here and work for me," the Duchess went on. "I have several ideas about musical instruments that I want you to execute."

Sebastien bowed low. But he hesitated. "A workshop, your Grace, is a necessity for that kind of work."

The Duchess brushed aside his objection. "An apartment will be fitted up here for you. Tools, materials, everything you need shall be supplied. And it goes without saying that you shall be suitably rewarded."

Still Sebastien hesitated. It was a great temptation, of course. But to have to work always on someone else's plans, when he had so many ideas of his own he wanted to try out, when he was constantly coming across things that excited his curiosity and challenged his ingenuity . . .

The Duchess was watching him closely. "And of course," she added casually, "you will have plenty of time to work on projects of your own. You will be absolutely free."

That settled it. What more could a young fellow want? Sebastien Erard accepted her offer gratefully—with the stipulation that the arrangement would be temporary—and moved to the chateau immediately.

In the years that followed, Sebastien not only executed the designs of his patroness to her satisfaction but did much experimenting and designing of his own. When he saw a new pianoforte that had been imported into France, he recognized it as an instrument with a future. He studied the mechanism and figured out several improvements. As was his custom, he made many sketches of his ideas and built several models. Later on, when the Duchess expressed a desire for a pianoforte, Sebastien found no difficulty in building one. In 1777 this pianoforte, the first ever made in France, was finished. The Duchess was delighted with it and praised it to all her friends. Sebastien received many orders for pianofortes.

The young craftsman was now so certain of his ability as designer and builder of instruments that he persuaded the Duchess to release him, and sent for his brother Jean-Baptiste. Together the Erard brothers started an instrument factory in Paris, in the Rue Bourbon. (The firm is still in business, and to this day enjoys a fine reputation.)

Everything went well at first. Business prospered. Their pianofortes were in great demand. The brothers had all the work they could do.

But their success aroused the jealousy of rival instrument firms, who watched for a chance to put them out of business. It was not long before an opportunity presented itself.

In those days luthiers (instrument makers) were accustomed to ornament their work with mother-of-pearl mosaics and other extravagant decorations, and so they were supposed to belong to the so-called Fanmakers' Guild. When Parisian luthiers learned that the Erard brothers were not registered members of the guild, they brought suit against them.

This meant trouble, indeed, for Sebastien and his brother. If they lost the lawsuit, they would be out of business. . . . And how could they win? How could they justify their failure to comply with Paris customs?

Help came from an unexpected source: no less a personage than the King of France, Louis XVI, who had found the Erard pianoforte a superb instrument. He conferred a medal on Sebastien, honoring his work in instrument making, and gave the brothers a special dispensation to continue their work without joining the Guild, providing they employed only workmen who satisfied the Guild's requirements.

So the lawsuit was settled, and the Erard business boomed. The brothers made a tremendous number of pianofortes. Sebastien continued to work on improvements for the instrument, as his inquiring mind saw the reasons for its various weaknesses. Also he invented a combination piano-organ, and even made a contrivance for the queen, Marie Antoinette, by which the instrument could be transposed to fit the range of her voice.

About this time Sebastien became interested in the harp, which was becoming more and more popular in France. Certainly that instrument needed improving as much as the pianoforte—possibly more so. About a hundred years before, tuning hooks had been added to the neck of the primitive harp, close to the upper ends of the strings, so that each string could be raised a semitone by making the hook nip the string. The trouble was, the mechanism pulled the strings out of the vertical plane, and the resulting tones were not good. Moreover, the harpist had to stop playing to tune a string, and the instrument could not play in all keys.

Several men, Sebastien knew, had worked on the harp since then, trying to make it useful for all keys. About 1720 Hochbrucker, the Bavarian, had designed pedals to actuate the hooks. His harp had five foot pedals, which shortened the C, D, F, G, and A strings a semitone. But the quality of the stopped notes was still poor, and the entire mechanism was flimsy. This harp did not prove satisfactory.

Then there was the harp of Simon, of Brussels, which was made chromatic by adding more strings. Seventy-eight strings! How difficult it must have been to play! And there was the pedal harp of Cousineau, the Frenchman. It could play in nearly all keys, but it had fourteen pedals! How could two feet be expected to operate fourteen pedals fast enough for smooth and true playing?

No, Sebastien Erard was sure that the secret of making the harp playable in all keys, and at the same time easy to operate, had not yet been found.

Sebastien's interest in the harp was stimulated by his growing friendship with Johann Baptist Krumpholtz, a noted Hungarian harpist and composer for the instrument.

One day Krumpholtz said to his friend, "You are so clever at making things. I wish you would make something for me, Sebastien."

"Why, certainly, my friend," Erard answered. "I'll make anything you like."

"I want a double-bass keyboard instrument that can be played with the feet," Krumpholtz told him. "I want to put it under my harp and play an accompaniment with my feet while I perform on the harp."

Sebastien Erard saw nothing strange in this request. All his life he had been making things no one else had ever done. His active mind began to formulate plans for the new instrument. Quickly he sketched his ideas. Then he made a model. Before long he presented the finished instrument to his friend.

"Wonderful!" Krumpholtz cried. "Exactly what I wanted." And he proceeded to play both the harp and the pedal keyboard at the same time.

Suddenly he stopped and looked at the inventor. "Why don't you do something about the harp? It is so easy for you to make things, I should think you could make a harp that would give the same clear tone when the strings are stopped as when they are open."

"I've been thinking about the harp for some time," Erard admitted. "I'll see what I can do."

He soon came to the conclusion that the plan of construction of all existing harps was wrong; the strings should be shortened without pulling them out of the perpendicular. New ideas began to come to him, and as usual he put them down on paper. Before long he had made a model for a harp conceived on an entirely new principle—one which had no hooks at all. The stopped notes were as clear as the open ones.

Confident of his course now, Sebastien began the manufacture of this new harp.

When word of this got around, people tried to discourage him. The French playwright, Beaumarchais, came to him and told him he was wasting his time and his money; he, himself, had tried to make a better harp, Beaumarchais said, but it could not be done.

Rival harp-makers tried to dissuade Erard for more selfish reasons; they knew that if he succeeded with a hookless harp, their products would not sell. They persuaded Krumpholtz to try to get the Erard brothers to drop the harp project.

Sebastien and Jean-Baptiste listened patiently to what Krumpholtz had to say. The harpist found his mission embarrassing because he had been the one to persuade Sebastien to start work on the harp in the first place. But neither of the Erards mentioned this.

The brothers would not promise to destroy their new-type harps. But they did agree to put them aside, temporarily, unfinished. (They had about fifty under construction in their factory.) They would delay launching their harp on the market until they had thought the matter over carefully.

While the Erards were still trying to decide what to do, the French Revolution started, and no decision was necessary. Harp and pianoforte factories alike closed down. All industry came to a standstill.

But Sebastien could not remain idle. He determined to go to London. Perhaps he could go into the harp business there without injuring Paris harp-makers. At least he could find out what was being done in England.

Erard spent ten years in England. He started a factory there, and he spent much time in experimenting, working out improvements and perfecting his harp mechanism.

When he returned to France in 1796, after the Reign of Terror, he opened his factory again and launched his single-action pedal harp. It was a distinct advance over previous models, but it did not satisfy Sebastien. It could not command all keys and all notes. If the A strings were sharped, there was no A natural, and so on. Except for the sturdiness of its construction and the improved quality of the stopped notes, the instrument was not much better, after all, than Hochbrucker's old model.

Sebastien thought about the problem long and earnestly. He covered page after page with sketches, only to tear them all up. What was really needed, he knew, was two pedals for each note of the scale, like Cousineau had used: one to raise the string a half tone, and one to raise it a whole tone. But seven pedals are as many as two feet can handle adequately. What could be done about it?

For several years the problem obsessed Sebastien Erard. Sometimes he worked night and day, experimenting, making model after model. For at least three months he did not undress, but slept a few hours at a time on a sofa in his workshop. If he had not inherited from his father a strong constitution, he could not have stood the long grueling work.

Frequently he was tempted to give up. Perhaps Beaumarchais was right, after all; perhaps a better harp could not be made. But his brother's faith in him, and his own inquisitive mind would not let him give up. He kept on trying.

And suddenly the solution was plain: give each pedal two jobs to do!

That, indeed, was the answer. Though it was far from easy to put this simple plan into operation, Sebastien Erard succeeded at last in constructing a double-action pedal harp. Each pedal had two positions: when it was depressed to the first position its strings were shortened by half a tone, and when it was pushed all the way down, the strings were shortened a full tone. Each pedal, of course, tuned all the strings of its note through all the octaves.

The Erards brought out the new double-action harp in 1811. Its success was immediate and gratifying. In one year the Erard firm sold 25,000 pounds (well over $100,000) worth of harps. Best of all, the harp was enabled to take its place as an instrument of grace and beauty, capable of being played in any key—an instrument, in short, which is a worthy culmination of the harp's long and varied career.

PART TWO

Music from Pipes

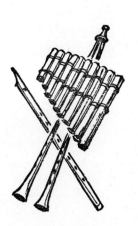

WHEN Primitive Man, thousands of years ago, crept through the forests with his hunting bow (which fathered our stringed instruments) he heard the wind rustling through reeds and grasses. Sometimes he noticed a musical sound, and if he investigated, he found that the sound came from a broken reed where the wind blew over the open tube.

Later, at his leisure, he broke a reed and blew across the end. To his delight, he found that he could duplicate the music of the wind. Soon he discovered that the pitch of the whistle varied with the length of his reed.

Primitive Man had learned two more things about tone production:

(1) *The column of air inside a tube can be made to vibrate, giving off a musical sound.*

(2) *The shorter the tube, the higher the pitch of the tone.*

He did not know that the higher pitch was due, not to the shortness of the tube, but to the faster vibrations of the column of air, caused by shortening the pipe.

Primitive Man had taken the first step in the development of our woodwind instruments.

49

Shortening Holes

1. An open pipe without shortening holes, or with the holes closed.

Bell 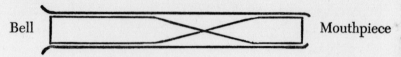 Mouthpiece

The sound wave travels from the mouthpiece to the bell and back again to give the fundamental tone.

2. An open pipe with one shortening hole open.

Bell 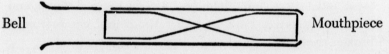 Mouthpiece

When a shortening hole is opened, the sound wave travels only as far as the hole and back to the mouthpiece, giving a higher fundamental because the length of the sound wave is shorter.

Without Reeds

Another family in the symphony orchestra is called the woodwinds. Like the string section, this family has four regular members: flute, clarinet, oboe, and bassoon. Occasionally a piccolo (little brother to the flute) and an English horn (or alto oboe) are added, and once in a while a saxophone.

When Primitive Man first discovered the reed whistle, he was content for a while to play the single note (called the fundamental tone) which each length of pipe produced naturally. Then he found that by varying his method of blowing he could obtain from each pipe certain higher notes; we call these *harmonics*, and we know today that they are caused by splitting the column of air and making it vibrate in sections.

Later, Primitive Man learned that a hole bored in the side of his pipe made the tone higher. By covering the hole with his finger he could still produce the pipe's fundamental tone and its harmonics, as well as the new tone and *its* harmonics. He had discovered two more principles of tone production:

(1) *In any open pipe of a given length, the air column has a certain pitch when it vibrates as a whole. This pitch is called the fundamental note of the pipe.*

(2) *If the column of air is shortened, by cutting off the pipe, or by opening a hole in the pipe, the length of the vibrations is shortened and the resulting pitch is higher.*

Gradually more holes were added, as many as there were fingers to cover them, and the woodwinds were on the way to becoming real instruments.

6. Extra Fingers Needed

Like the primitive hunter's broken reed, the flute is a pipe, although today it is usually made of silver. In place of blowing across the end of the tube, the player blows across a hole which is placed near the end; his breath sets in motion the column of air inside the tube, and the result is a musical tone.

The silver-voiced flute is often called the "coloratura soprano of the woodwinds" because of the spectacular trills and runs it can perform. Excepting the violin, it is the most versatile and agile of all instruments.

But this was not always true. Although the flute can trace its ancestry back to the simple reed whistle of the cave man, in its present form it is little more than a hundred years old. Unlike most instruments, whose modern perfection is due to the contributions of many people, the flute owes so much to a single man that his name is inseparably linked with it. Nearly seventy years of his long and active life were devoted to the improvement of his beloved flute.

In the spring of 1831 Theobald Boehm, flutist in the Royal Bavarian Orchestra of Munich, arrived in London on a concert tour. He had been looking forward to London for a long time. No city presented more of a challenge to a flutist, for England was extremely flute-conscious in those days. Thousands of flutes were being made and sold. The instrument was played by countless amateurs as well as by professionals.

However, Boehm was not unduly concerned about his forthcoming performances. In his native Germany he was considered the best flutist of his time, noted for beautiful, pure tones and sympathetic interpretation. Although far from vain, Boehm felt confident that he could compete with the best flutists London might offer.

Much of his confidence came from the instrument he used, one of his own manufacture. For nearly twenty years, off and on, he had been making flutes, striving always to improve them, and now he had his own little flute factory in Munich. He was certain that this eight-keyed flute, with pillars to support the keys, would prove superior to the English models.

And so it seemed at first. On May 9th, when Boehm played his own composition, *Grand Polonaise in D*, at the London

Philharmonic concert, the applause was highly gratifying. A few weeks later, his solos at Moschelles' concert drew equal praise. Boehm felt well satisfied with the performance of his instrument.

Then occurred an incident which proved to be a milestone in his life, and which had a far-reaching effect on the instrument he loved. Theobald Boehm, flutist, went on a sort of "busman's holiday" and attended a concert featuring Charles Nicholson, the famous English flutist.

At the very first notes, Boehm sat up straight, tense with amazement. What power! What volume! Never had he heard such full tones from a flute. The tone of his own flute, though sweet and pure, was not powerful; it could not begin to match this man's flute. The German musician could hardly wait until the end of the concert; he wanted to see that remarkable instrument.

As the last number ended, Boehm rushed backstage. The soloist, a big handsome man, was already surrounded by admirers. Boehm had to wait some minutes before he could introduce himself and offer his congratulations. He listened impatiently to Nicholson's compliments on his own London performances.

"Your flute," said Boehm as soon as the courtesies were over. "May I see it, please?"

"Certainly," answered Nicholson, handing him the instrument. New arrivals claimed the soloist's attention just then, and Boehm was free to examine the Englishman's flute.

Like his own, it was made of cocus wood, though not so finely finished. It lacked many of the improvements his own instrument had. The keys were not so well made. The holes were unevenly placed and of unequal size. Yet its tone was far more powerful than his own.

At once Boehm saw the secret of the big tone: the holes were very large; some were so big his own fingers could not cover them.

With a word of thanks, Boehm returned the flute to its owner and made his way out of the building. As he walked he looked down at his own long thin fingers and sighed. Never in the world could he play a flute with holes of that diameter. Yet if large holes were necessary for powerful tone . . . Boehm could not dismiss the subject from his mind.

A few days later the German called on the London firm of Gerock and Wolf, instrument makers, at 79 Cornhill. He left specifications for a flute which would embody several ideas that had come to him since seeing Nicholson's flute, including slightly larger holes.

Shortly before his final London performance in June, Boehm was approached by another flute enthusiast, Captain William Gordon, from Paris. He, too, had been working for years to improve the instrument; in fact, he was in London now hoping to patent his new model and interest some firm in manufacturing it.

Boehm and Gordon showed each other their instruments and held long discussions on the relative merits of various keys and materials. Boehm admired the ingenuity of Gordon's keys and levers; he had adopted the ring-key invented by the Reverend Frederick Nolan of England. Boehm had long been considering the use of ring-keys; he felt, however, that the captain's instrument was too complicated to be a success. On the other hand, he was not too pleased with his own latest model when Gerock and Wolf finally delivered it.

No, the ideal flute had not yet been made. Each flute had something: Nicholson's had volume, Gordon's had a good idea in its keys, his own had pure tone. But none of them had everything.

"Vague experimenting," Boehm told Gordon, "will never lead to a real improvement of the flute. Without a change in the present fingering, the instrument will never be equalized in tone. Nicholson's flute has set me to thinking. . . ."

Boehm reached his home in Munich in September of 1831. His tour had been a grand success. The townspeople hastened to do him honor. The King increased his salary. But Boehm took all the praise and feting with a feeling of deep humility and even a touch of impatience. He had come to a momentous decision and he wanted to carry it out. As soon as he could he told the chief workmen of his little factory about his plan.

"Gréve, I'm going to discard my old flute and start over."

"Discard it!" cried Gréve in dismay.

Boehm nodded firmly. "Yes. I've decided that a flute must have large note-holes, fairly uniform in size, and placed so that they give correct tones regardless of whether the fingers can reach them or not."

Gréve's mouth dropped open. "But if the fingers cannot reach the holes, how can the flute be played?"

Boehm shrugged. "We'll worry about that later. The important thing is to find the correct size and placement of the holes, to ensure true, powerful tones."

As Boehm rolled up his sleeves ready to work, his assistant shook his head ruefully. "We're already making the best flutes in Germany, Herr Boem," he protested. "Why worry about making better ones?"

Theobald Boehm paid no attention. He was already preparing for his first experiment.

First he made several identical wooden flutes of the slightly conical type which had been in use for many years. He put no holes in them except the blow-hole, or embouchure. He blew into each one in turn; all gave the same tone. Satisfied, he nodded.

Then Boehm cut off the end of one flute, little by little, constantly testing its tone, until the sound was a full tone above the others. Carefully he measured on the shortened flute the distance from the embouchure to the end of the tube; on a second flute he marked the spot for a hole exactly the same distance from its blow-hole.

Taking up the experimental flute again, he cut off the tube a bit at a time until it was the right length for the next tone of the scale. Again he measured, and again he marked a hole in flute number two.

Hour after hour, day after day, the work went on. Gréve hovered around, anxious to help; but there was little he could do. Boehm would trust no eye but his own on the measurement, no lips but his own to test the tones.

When at last he finished this part of his work, the experimental flute was a mere stub. Then he cut the holes in flute number two. Fourteen holes, all of the same fairly large size and spaced along the tube for accurate intonation. . . .

But the pitches were not accurate, after all. A hole, Boehm found to his dismay, does not shorten the column of air in the flute tube as effectively as cutting off the tube at that point.

He would have to begin all over.

Taking two more tubes, he started the same routine of test-ing and cutting and measuring. But this time he cut each hole in the second flute as he marked it. If the tone was not true he discarded that tube and took another, moving the hole slightly closer to the embouchure.

This time when he finished, the results were better. His flute's tones were not absolutely true, but they were far more accurate than any previous instrument he had heard, and they were sweet and powerful.

His assistant eyed the new flute dubiously. "No one can play it, Herr Boehm. No one can ever finger that flute. How can you cover fourteen holes with only nine fingers, espe-cially when some of those holes are out of reach? The right thumb must support the instrument, you know."

Boehm smiled. His brown eyes sparkled. "I have a couple of ideas on that point, Gréve. In London I saw a flute with ring-keys. It was crude, and too complicated in design, but basically, I believe, the solution of our problem."

For many weeks Boehm worked on the key-mechanism plan of his new flute. He made sketches of several different plans, but he could not decide which was best. At last he built three flutes, each with a different key system, and tested them thoroughly in actual practice.

In the end he settled on an open-key system because open keys could be worked faster and more easily than closed keys. Closed keys required stiff springs if they were not to leak, while light springs were sufficient for open keys.

As Boehm had hoped, he found in the ring-key the answer to the crucial question Gréve had raised: how could nine fingers cover fourteen holes at once? A ring-key, as Boehm made it, was really two keys mounted on the same axle, one with a pad and the other with a ring. A finger pressing the ring could cover one hole and at the same time the pad covered a second hole which was out of reach. Thus one finger could cover two holes, and nine fingers were more than enough for fourteen holes. The upper six holes, as on all flutes of the time, were to be covered by the fingers, and the lower ones closed by keys.

When it was finished in December of 1832, Boehm's new flute proved to be the best yet produced in power, trueness of tone, and ease of operation. It did not become instantly popular, however, because the new key system necessitated entirely different fingering from the old-style flutes, so that a player had to learn all over again.

Gradually, in spite of this drawback, the Boehm flute gained favor throughout the world. But as its popularity grew the maker himself became less and less satisfied with it. The tones were not really accurate and he would not be willing to rest on his laurels until the flute was as perfect as human hands could make it.

After several years of activity in other lines connected with his trade as a goldsmith, Boehm went back to the study of the problem of improving the flute. He soon decided that he must learn more about acoustics. He must attack the problem of flute-making scientifically.

Accordingly Boehm took up the study of acoustics with his friend, Dr. Carl von Schafhäutl, of the Bavarian University, determined to make an acoustically correct instrument. Over a period of several years he conducted more than three hundred experiments to ascertain the best possible size and shape and material for a flute.

Eventually Boehm made, with his own hands, a flute which was radically different from any previous model. It was fashioned of a different material: silver instead of wood. It had a different shape: cylindrical except for the head joint (the same shape which is used today). All the dimensions, toneholes, etc., were decided on the basis of the laws of acoustics, and not on the basis of convenience for the fingers. It kept the same key-system and fingering of the 1832 model, except that all holes—which were very much larger: too large to be closed by fingers—were of necessity covered by pads. No ring-keys were used.

The key-mechanism was so delicately and accurately made that the keys worked as smoothly as the finest clock mechanism; the performer could cover a hole which was out of reach of his fingers (and too large to be covered by a finger, anyway) as perfectly as if the hole were half its size and lay right under his hand.

This new Boehm flute, completed in 1847, had fifteen toneholes and twenty-three keys and levers; it produced tones so true, so pure and sweet and powerful, that the instrument has scarcely been improved to this day. Hence it is no wonder that the name "Boehm" has come to be associated inseparably with the flute, to which Theobald Boehm dedicated his life.

Double Reeds

While he was experimenting with the musical possibilities of various reeds and pipes, Primitive Man made another momentous discovery.

One day he was playing idly with a thin reed, perhaps sucking water through it, or blowing through it as a child blows soap bubbles. Suddenly he noticed that no air or water would go through; one end, soaking wet, had collapsed.

Primitive Man put the flattened end of the reed into his mouth and blew hard, trying to force the tube open. Nothing happened. He tried different ways of blowing. Finally he blew a very thin stream of air, and the collapsed reed vibrated, giving off a musical sound.

He had discovered the basic principle of double-reed instruments:

> *A thin stream of air forced between two reeds will set in motion the air column inside a pipe, causing vibrations which produce a musical tone.*

Later on he found that a conical tube worked better than a cylindrical one, and that two separate reeds tied onto the pipe made a more satisfactory mouthpiece.

The double-reed woodwinds were on their way.

7. Snake Charmer's Descendant

There is an absurd superstition that playing the oboe may drive you insane. Like most superstitions, this one probably was founded on a coincidence. Playing the oboe is no more likely to lead to insanity than playing any other instrument.

But there is no doubt that the oboe is a difficult and maddening instrument. So little air can be used in producing a tone that playing the oboe is practically like holding the breath. A player must have frequent rests, not so much so that he can breathe air into his lungs as to allow him to breathe *out* the stale air.

The crude ancestor of the oboe, the double-reed shawm, had been used in the Orient for thousands of years before Europeans became acquainted with it. During the Crusades, in the eleventh and twelfth centuries, Europeans saw and heard this instrument for the first time. As they traveled toward Jerusalem and fought with the Turks, they heard the thin reedy music of the shawm on every hand. In religious rites, in social affairs, in military activities, the penetrating voice of the shawm predominated.

The shawm was the stand-by of the magician, too. His best tricks were done to the accompaniment of its high, haunting music. The oriental fakir could make ladders materialize, cause people to disappear, and charm snakes with the distinctive music of the double-reed shawm as tool or prop.

Like the snakes, the Crusaders felt the mesmerizing influence of the reedy shawm. They carried the instrument back with them to Europe. Before long it had penetrated into every country of the civilized world.

By the time that the symphony orchestra began to evolve, early in the seventeenth century, the shawm (much improved now) was made in many different sizes. The higher pitched one, called "hautbois" or "high wood instrument," as opposed to the lower pitched one, was such an important instrument of that day that it was included in the early orchestra as a matter of course. Its tone was loud and strident.

Like the flute, the oboe had begun to use shortening holes to cut down its column of air and thus add more notes to its scale. When keys began to be added to the flute, the oboe followed suit. But what worked well on the flute was not always successful on the more delicate and complicated oboe.

Only the flute and the drums are older than the oboe. Only the violin has had a longer life in the orchestra. Yet the oboe was the last of the standard orchestra instruments to be modernized.

Charles Triebert had been brought up in an atmosphere of double-reed instruments. His father, a German who became a naturalized Frenchman, was a well-known maker of oboes and bassoons. Both Charles and his younger brother Frederic had helped their father in his shop from the time they could remember, and they had learned to play the oboe as soon as their fingers were big enough to cover the holes.

There was no question of any other career for Charles but that of oboist. As soon as he was old enough he was enrolled in the Paris Conservatoire. In 1829, when he was nineteen, he took first prize in oboe. His family was proud of him, but the honor was no more than they had expected. Any Triebert should be outstanding on the oboe.

Soon after his graduation from the Conservatoire, Charles Triebert was admitted to the orchestra of the Opera Comique in Paris, to take the place of Apollon Marie Barret who had left that orchestra to play in London.

Although he was delighted to obtain the position in the

orchestra, Charles was sorry to see Barret leave Paris. Barret, too, had been a prize-winning oboist at the Conservatoire. He, too, had been a pupil of the famous oboe professor, Gustave Vogt. Charles Triebert had heard much during his years of study with Vogt about the remarkable talent of Apollon Barret, and he had often gone to the theater to hear him play. It was quite natural that Charles' admiration of the somewhat older Barret should be second only to his veneration for their teacher, Vogt.

Several years passed. Charles Triebert was making a reputation for himself in Paris as an oboist, as Apollon Barret was doing in London. The elder Triebert continued to make oboes and bassoons. Both of his sons helped him as of old; for Charles it was a spare time occupation, when he was not busy with orchestra or concert work, but for Frederic, now grown, the shop had become the chief concern. Due to the combined efforts of the three, Triebert oboes were becoming known as the very best on the market in Western Europe. Orders came from many cities in France and England, especially from London where Barret had spread the fame of the Tribert oboe. The firm of Triebert and Sons should have a secure and easy future.

But something happened in 1832 which was destined to have a tremendous effect on the Triebert oboe shop, and make them work harder than they had ever worked in their lives. Theobald Boehm brought out his new flute with its revolutionary key mechanism.

The Trieberts paid little attention to the controversy that raged as to whether Boehm had really invented the mechanism himself or had stolen the idea from Captain Gordon of the King's Swiss Guards. All that the oboe-obsessed family had ears for were the unanimous cries of joy from flutists who had the courage and the patience to master the fingering of the new instrument: they were unanimous in their praise of the flute's tone; Boehm's key mechanism had improved the instrument a hundred per cent.

The Trieberts were fully aware of the deficiencies of the oboe. All woodwinds were faulty; it was inevitable that some tones should be off-key, and that many passages of music should be almost impossible to finger. After all, one could not expect a single instrument to be able to play *everything*. They had been content to make minor improvements and refinements in the oboe as the years went on, never dreaming of the possibility of a radical reformation such as this man Boehm had done on the flute.

But now . . . If such a thing could be done for the flute, why not the oboe, too?

"We'll do it!" cried Charles. "We'll use the same key system on the oboe."

His father shook his head doubtfully. "I don't think it will work."

But Charles was confident. "Of course, it will. Ring-keys! That's the answer to all our problems."

Fired by the enthusiasm of Charles, the three Trieberts began to work on a key mechanism for the oboe. Months of work followed, but they did not succeed in transplanting the Boehm mechanism to the oboe. At last even Charles was forced to admit that the system in its entirety could not be used.

But Charles would not quit. Just because they could not

use the whole system did not mean they could not utilize parts of it.

By this time Apollon Barret in London had heard what Charles Triebert was trying to do. He greeted the project of the younger oboist with delight, and offered many suggestions.

Thus there grew up a sort of long-distance collaboration, with Barret suggesting mechanical improvements on the oboe and the Trieberts, inspired by Charles, carrying them out.

It took many years to complete the Barret-Triebert reformation of the oboe. It was no startling, radical change they made, such as Boehm had done on the flute, and Klosé on the clarinet. Rather, it was a slow, careful succession of gradual changes: rod-axles for the little-finger keys, different placement for certain holes, modification of the shake keys, a single fingerplate for two or more keys, a double automatic octave key, and so on. They used Boehm's ring-keys, Buffet's needle springs and clutches, and some ideas of their own. The system was characterized by its great number of alternate fingerings, making many difficult passages much easier to play.

Twenty years from the time that Boehm's first sensational flute had appeared, Apollon Barret and Charles Triebert were ready to say that the oboe was as perfect as their combined efforts could make it. In 1855 Triebert entered one of their new oboes in the Paris Exhibition and received a medal on it.

Barret wrote and published a method for the new oboe, calling it, *A Complete Method, Comprising All New Fingering, Scales, and Shakes.* He also published several pieces for the instrument.

Although many Frenchmen and many Germans, both before and after them (particularly Gillet), contributed to the perfection of the oboe, Charles Triebert and Apollon Barret stand out as the most persistent of all who devoted their energies to the development of that descendant of the oriental fakir's snake-charmer, the oboe.

8. Three-Sided Collaboration

Have you ever noticed the long wooden instrument in the orchestra that looks like a couple of poles tied together, with a thin curved tongue sticking out about a third of the way from the top? That is the bassoon, whose name means "big bass of the woodwinds."

Since the fundamental pitch of a wind instrument depends

on the length of its tube (the longer the tube, the deeper the pitch), the bass naturally requires a very long tube. When the first bass woodwinds were made they were stretched out straight like the flute and clarinet and oboe. It took a tube about eight feet long to produce the low notes musicians wanted; two men were needed to carry around and play the long bass instrument. This, of course, was inconvenient and unsatisfactory. A way had to be found to shorten the bass woodwind. Unlike metal, wood can not be twisted or coiled to make a long instrument easy to handle, and the bass woodwinds did not sound like themselves when made of metal.

Early in the sixteenth century a churchman, Afranio of Ferrara, found a way out of this difficulty: he laid two wooden cylinders side by side and connected them, U-fashion, at the bottom. That was the beginning of the characteristic bassoon shape, although Afranio's instrument was more like a bagpipe than a modern bassoon.

For three hundred years the bassoon developed slowly, adding note-holes and keys. But the fingering remained so difficult and the tones so uncertain and unequal that it was given little to do in the orchestra. The bassoon seemed likely to be the lame duck of the orchestra if it could not keep pace with the other woodwinds in mechanical improvements.

Finally a man who was a bassoon player, conductor and composer set himself the task of correcting some of the faults of his favorite instrument.

In 1816 the German, Karl Almenrader, finished his service as regimental bandmaster in the Napoleonic Wars. His had been a varied career; although he was barely out of his twenties, he could boast more kinds of musical experience than most men encounter in a lifetime. Before his army enlistment, he had been professor of bassoon at the Cologne Music School, and then a member of the theater orchestra at Frankfort-on-Main. Now he accepted the post of bandmaster in Mainz.

Almenrader enjoyed directing the band. But that was not enough. He wanted to make music himself, not just conduct the music of others.

As long as he could remember, music had been a part of him. His father, a town musician of Dusseldorf, had taught him the elements of music when he was little more than a baby. He had learned to play the harpsichord, the flute and the horn. And then, when he was thirteen, somebody gave him a bassoon.

Karl Almenrader smiled, remembering that first bassoon of his. What a poor excuse for an instrument it had been! But he had loved it. From his first tentative trials, Almenrader had recognized that the deep-voiced bassoon was the instrument for him. He forsook all other music for the study of the bassoon, and it had been his love ever since. He felt he was only half-living if he was not playing his beloved instrument.

So now, in Mainz, Germany, in 1816, he determined to find out if there was an opening for a bassoon player in an orchestra or chamber group. He thought himself in luck when he obtained a place in the theater orchestra of Mainz. But the orchestra thought *themselves* in luck. Good bassoon players, then as now, were scarce. In fact, they had never had one of Almenrader's caliber. The theater manager was particularly impressed with the new bassoonist, and so was Gottfried

Weber, composer and musical theorist of Mainz, as well as substitute conductor of the orchestra.

For years Weber had been studying the acoustics of music. He had recently published a pamphlet on his findings, called, *Akustik der Blasinstrumente*. It delighted him to find in Karl Almenrader an intelligent and sympathetic listener to his theories. The two men had many long talks on the subject of music.

While he loved the deep-voiced bassoon above all other instruments, Almenrader recognized its many faults. Especially he had always deplored the off-key tones that seemed inevitable in such a long instrument. A bassoonist expended most of his energy correcting his intonation.

The theories of Weber opened Almenrader's eyes to the causes of the bassoon's worst defects. Why, the holes weren't properly placed, and many of them were not the right size. Almost at once Almenrader came to a decision: he would embark on a scientific study of bassoon-making.

But he had no workshop. And he did not have the necessary tools and materials. Furthermore, he would not know how to use these things if he had them; he was a musician, not a mechanic. He must enlist some instrument maker in his project.

The firm of B. Schott-Söhne of Mainz, anxious to better their instruments, agreed to let Karl Almenrader carry on his experiments in their factory, and assigned a workman to help him.

Guided by Weber's theories of acoustics, Almenrader worked for years, studying, experimenting, and testing. At last, in 1820, he finished working out specifications for a fifteen-keyed bassoon which should be acoustically correct. He published his findings in a treatise describing it, and Schott-Söhne built several instruments to his order.

The keys of the new bassoon were curved to fit the rounded surface of the tube; instead of flat leather, there were stuffed pads under the key covers. The size and situation of many of the note-holes were different from those of the old instrument. There were several additional tones at the top of the scale. All in all, it was a vastly improved bassoon, its tones far truer and more uniform.

Before long the growing demand for his new bassoon prompted Almenrader to go into the business of manufacturing them. He opened a small factory in Cologne and began to build bassoons. But the work of running the factory was too much for him; his health had never been robust, and the unaccustomed factory work took a great toll of his strength. He was forced to give up the business after two years, and he handed over to the Schott firm the responsibility of turning out the new bassoon.

Then Almenrader went to Biebrich as first bassoonist in the orchestra of the Duke of Nasseau, but he continued to supervise the production of bassoons in the Schott factory, always trying to improve the instruments.

One of the most intelligent and capable of the Schott workmen was a young fellow named Johan Adam Heckel. After working on the bassoon for several years, under Almenrader's direction, Heckel became as obsessed as Almenrader with the idea of perfecting the instrument. Finally, in 1831 he joined Almenrader in Biebrich and set up in business there as a bassoon-maker. Almenrader, still advised by Weber, continued to give him suggestions for improvements.

As the years passed the Heckel bassoon, made in accordance with Almenrader's ideas and based on Weber's theories of acoustics, became known as the best on the market. And Almenrader himself gained fame as the best bassoonist in Germany, as well as author of an excellent instruction book, and composer of considerable music, both solos and ensembles pieces, for the "Big Bass of the Woodwinds."

Single Reeds

Long, long after the reed pipe was discovered, and long after the double-reed shawm was developed, Primitive Man made another discovery. As he played on a crude cane flute, he noted a different quality to the tone: a thin, reedy sound. When he examined his instrument to determine the cause, he found that a portion of the cane had split and was vibrating as he blew into the pipe. Inadvertently he had made a new instrument!

Quite by accident this man, whoever he was, had discovered a new thing about tone production:

A thin sliver of cane or reed, made to flutter by the breath, sets the air column inside a pipe to vibrating and gives a distinctive musical sound.

He had begun the development of the single-reed wood-winds.

9. *It Couldn't Be Done*

As the violin is the heart of the symphony orchestra, so **is** the clarinet the heart of the wind-band. It plays the lead **in** the band just as the violin does in the orchestra.

The clarinet is an instrument of extremes:

It is the *least tunable* of all orchestra instruments.

It is the *most sensitive* to heat and cold.

It has the *greatest range* of all woodwinds.

It was the *last* instrument to enter the classical orchestra.

And it was the *most difficult* instrument to fit with a satisfactory key system. In fact, the experts said it couldn't be done at all.

In 1840 Hyacinthe Eléanore Klosé had been professor of clarinet at the Paris Conservatoire for a year. Staff and students alike were pleased with him. He was a good teacher; he had had years of experience as a bandmaster in the army; and he was considered one of the greatest clarinet soloists of his day.

But Klosé was not pleased with himself. Although he worked diligently with his students and kept up his own practising faithfully, he could not get the results he wanted. Better tone, smoother performance—these were the things he must achieve. But he could not obtain these results, either from his students or himself.

At last Klosé came to the conclusion that the fault lay in the clarinet itself. The instrument should have more resonance, and the tones should be more accurate. Moreover, certain key signatures were very difficult to play in, and some trills were utterly impossible. He must find a better make of clarinet.

The professor went to shop after shop. But when he asked for a better clarinet than the one he had, instrument makers were astounded at the request.

"Why, you have the best clarinet that was ever made, Professor Klosé!" one manufacturer told him. "A thirteen-keyed Müller. It is a great improvement on previous instruments."

Klosé shrugged impatiently. He knew the history of his instrument: how J. C. Denner, an instrument maker of Nuremburg, had developed the clarinet from the old chalumeau (a simple pipe with a split reed mouthpiece), giving it a speaker key so it would overblow more easily, and adding holes to fill out the scale; how one man after another had added more keys until finally Ivan Müller had brought out this vastly improved thirteen-keyed clarinet. But it still wasn't good enough.

Klosé pointed to a flute on the counter. "That's a Boehm flute, isn't it?"

The instrument maker nodded. "Yes. That is, we use Boehm's key mechanism, with certain improvements that we Parisians have added."

Klosé picked up the flute. He had seen and heard the new Boehm flute (Boehm's first revolutionary flute of 1832) at the Paris Conservatoire, and had listened to many arguments about it: whether it was worth learning a new system of fingering for the sake of better tone quality; whether Boehm really deserved the credit for this new flute, or whether he had stolen the ideas from Gordon.

"Why can't we use this key system of Boehm's on the clarinet?" Klosé asked the instrument maker. "Why wouldn't it improve my instrument as much as it did the flute?"

"Impossible!" answered the other. "The clarinet and the flute are entirely different. On the flute you play up the scale and then you overblow the octave and go right on up. But on the clarinet—"

"I know," Klosé interrupted. "The flute is an open pipe, so it overblows to the octave. But the clarinet acts like a stopped pipe because its reed is so large as to practically cut off the air at the mouthpiece. In a stopped pipe the column of air must not only vibrate to the end of the pipe, but all the way back up again as well."

"Yes," agreed the instrument maker. "And a stopped pipe instrument overblows at the twelfth note instead of the eighth."

"That is why," nodded Klosé, "we must have more holes on the clarinet, to bridge the gap between the octave and the twelfth."

"Exactly!" The instrument maker's voice was triumphant. "And that is precisely why you cannot use the flute's key system on your clarinet. There are already twenty-two holes on this instrument of yours. What you suggest, professor—using Boehm's key system—would require many more holes on the clarinet. The key mechanism would have to be too big and too complicated."

Klosé left the shop and went on to another, only to be told substantially the same thing. But he was still not convinced. And he refused to give up his idea until he was absolutely certain it could not be done.

For many months, in the time he could spare from teaching and practising, Hyacinthe Klosé considered the problem, examining and testing both flutes and clarinets. At last he thought he saw how Boehm's key mechanism of the flute could be adapted to the clarinet.

But he could not do it himself; he was definitely no mechanic. And no instrument maker he asked would undertake the project. They all said it was impossible.

Finally Klosé took his plan to Auguste Buffet, Jr., who had made a number of improvements on the flute. And then he wondered why he had not gone to him before.

Amazingly, Buffet did not scoff at Klosé's idea as had everyone else. Instead, he considered the plan seriously.

"H'm. . . . Yes . . . It might work. . . . Difficult, of course, but few improvements are easy. . . . My new needle spring will be a great advantage on those keys. Also the sleeve I devised to permit reverse-acting keys to be mounted on the same axle . . . Yes, it might work. It is worth trying, monsieur."

To his great joy, Klosé soon found that Buffet was not only receptive to his radical ideas, but he was a genius at carrying them out. By 1843 Buffet had completed a new clarinet with the key mechanism which the clarinet professor had proposed.

The new instrument was everything Klosé had hoped for. It had *fewer* holes than his old Müller, instead of more, as the first instrument maker had predicted. Only eighteen note-holes. The tones were more uniform and true. The note-holes were placed more with regard to acoustics than finger-reach, and were controlled by an elaborate system of twenty-three keys, several of them ring-keys such as Boehm had used on his first flute. Any key signature was now readily playable, and practically all trills possible. On this clarinet much could be done that was very difficult, if not impossible, on the old instrument.

Of course, there was one disadvantage: like Boehm's flute, the new clarinet required drastic changes in fingering. A person who was used to playing the old instrument could not pick up the new one and become instantly expert on it. But once the new fingering had been mastered, this clarinet gave far greater satisfaction in tone quality and dexterity. Klosé was immensely pleased.

While Auguste Buffet obtained a patent on the new clarinet and went on to make more of them, Klosé mastered the technique of his improved instrument and then went on a concert tour throughout Europe to introduce it.

Everywhere he went people were amazed at his playing; but the necessary change of fingering kept his clarinet from being quickly and universally adopted. To help overcome this hesitancy, Klosé wrote an instruction book and had it published.

Eventually the Paris Conservatoire, seeing Klosé's success with his new instrument, gave official recognition to the "Boehm clarinet," as it was called (because Klosé's key system was based on Boehm's work). Gradually it gained favor and finally became generally accepted in most countries throughout the world.

Thus it was that Hyacinthe Klosé, the man who would not take the word of the experts that it couldn't be done, made it possible for the clarinet to become what it is today, the King of the Woodwinds. Although it is still not as perfect as the flute, it is far superior to the instrument Klosé and Buffet took in hand, and few improvements have been made on it since.

10. Experiment in Cross-Breeding

The saxophone is a bundle of contradictions. It looks very complicated, yet its mechanism is much simpler than the clarinet's or the oboe's. It is easy to learn to play it a little, but quite difficult to play well. It is made of brass, yet it is classed with the woodwinds, since it uses shortening-holes and keys like other woodwinds, instead of lengthening-tubes and valves, like the brasses.

The saxophone is one of the very few band or orchestra instruments that were actually invented, but it has not yet attained the place its inventor dreamed of for it: a regular place in the symphony orchestra.

In the spring of 1839, young Adolphe Sax of Brussels regretfully watched the great Habeneck, director of the opera orchestra in Paris, leave the Belgian capital after a short stay. How young Sax wished he were going to Paris with the famous conductor! Paris! There was a city for you. Life, color, music. Symphony, opera, the theater. That was the place in which he would like to live, instead of Brussels.

People in his home town took Adolphe's genius as a matter of course; they had paid little heed and less admiration to the fine instruments he had made in the years he had been working with his father in the instrument making business. And Belgians had been unimpressed with the new bass clarinet young Adolphe had recently invented. (There had been bass clarinets before, but his was such a complete reformation as to be really a new instrument.) No, there was no recognition for Adolphe Sax in Brussels.

In Paris, on the other hand, he would find appreciation. Habeneck had examined his bass clarinet and had complimented him highly on his ingenuity and skill.

"You'll make your mark in the world, young man," he had told him.

Of course, he would; Adolphe never doubted that—but it was nice to have others realize it, too.

But Paris was far away. Meantime, there was work to be done here in Brussels. There were ten other children in the family to be fed, and Adolphe, the eldest, must do his share.

He settled down philosophically to work in his father's shop, building such instruments as were ordered, and experimenting endlessly in his spare time, as was his habit.

Although he could play almost any instrument a little, and the flute and the clarinet well, Adolphe spent more time and thought on the clarinet than on all other instruments put together. This was partly because the clarinet had always held a special fascination for his father, and partly because its peculiar behavior intrigued Adolphe. The clarinet, alone of all wind instruments, refused to overblow to the octave. This necessitated a complicated mechanism to bridge the gap between the eighth of the scale and the twelfth, which was the first harmonic. Surely there must be some way to make a clarinet-type that would behave like other instruments, and so could have simpler mechanism.

One day Adolphe Sax was working with an ophicleide (a keyed serpent), a brass instrument of conical bore which was played with a cupped mouthpiece.

Suddenly he put it down and looked at his father, who was busy at an adjoining workbench. "I wonder what this ophicleide would sound like with a clarinet mouthpiece."

Charles Sax glanced up from his work. "A single-reed mouthpiece on a brass instrument? I don't know, Son. It has never been tried, so far as I know. A couple of men tried a reed mouthpiece on a *wooden* serpent, but brass . . . I don't know. Try it and see."

Fitting a beak-type mouthpiece to the ophicleide was no great task for a clever workman like Adolphe Sax. From early childhood he had been taught to use his hands; as a small youngster he had come into his father's shop and used his tools to make his own toys; at the age of six he could drill a clarinet body properly or twirl the cup of a horn; at sixteen he had made two flutes and a clarinet of ivory and had sent them to the Brussels Industrial Exhibition. So the small project of fitting a clarinet mouthpiece to a brass instrument, which was never intended for such an appendage, presented no problem at all.

When the mouthpiece was in place, Adolphe put it to his lips and breathed into it gently in approved clarinet fashion. And the sound that emerged amazed him! Instead of the harsh, loud tone of the ophicleide, or the sweet voice of the clarinet, it was something entirely new: slightly nasal and reedy, somewhat brassy, but mellow and powerful.

Charles Sax put down his tools and came to his son's side. "I believe you have an idea there, my Son. You have made a new kind of instrument, a link between the brasses and the woodwinds."

Deftly Adolphe moved his fingers over the keys, running up and down the scale; and he made a discovery that delighted him: this new hybrid instrument would overblow to the octave like the flute and the oboe, instead of to the twelfth like the clarinet!

With tremendous enthusiasm Adolphe Sax, encouraged and advised by his father, threw himself into the task of bringing this new instrument to perfection. The old ophicleide tube left much to be desired; he soon re-shaped it to his liking. The clarinet mouthpiece was too short; he made a new one, longer and slightly different in shape.

For months Sax made one instrument after another, always experimenting, always improving, at the same time keeping up his share of the regular work of the shop.

By the time the 1841 Belgian National Exhibition opened, Adolphe Sax had a showing of instruments to be proud of, including his bass clarinet, an improved regular clarinet, and his new instrument which he called the "saxophone." His exhibit would win a prize, Adolphe was confident. Except for his father, no instrument maker in Belgium could match him in fine workmanship. Besides, he was the only one with a brand new instrument.

The jury, however, refused Adolphe a prize. "Too young," they said.

Adolphe's fury knew no bounds. Too young, indeed! What did age have to do with ability? But the age was only an excuse, he knew; obviously the jury had been influenced. The jealousy of other instrument makers, no doubt.

It was the last straw. Adolphe Sax determined he would no longer stay in Brussels, to be ignored and rebuffed. He would go to Paris where his talents would be recognized.

A year later, in 1842, he set out for Paris, with no money, no income, no prospects, only a sample of his new instrument and unbounded confidence in his own ability as assets.

When he arrived in the French capital he had only thirty francs. For three days he had no food. He walked the streets, trying to get appointments with influential people, but it was not easy to find such people in or to get in to see them.

At last he managed to meet Hector Berlioz, the composer and critic, and showed him his instruments. Berlioz was enthusiastic.

"But this is wonderful!" he cried, when Sax had demonstrated his new invention. "This new—what do you call it?—

saxophone. The sound has a rare quality. Full, soft, vibrating, powerful. Yes, your saxophone is marvelous."

The critic was almost as effusive over Sax's other instruments, his bass clarinet and the trumpets he brought with him. To the hungry and weary Adolphe Sax the words of praise were better than meat and drink. Yes, he had done right in coming to Paris. Here he would find adequate appreciation of his ability.

Before the two parted, Berlioz had arranged for Sax to demonstrate his instruments at the Paris Conservatoire for several eminent musicians, including Meyerbeer and Halévy. And he had promised to mention Sax's instruments in his monthly column in the Paris *Journal des Debats.*

Sax walked away from Berlioz's door, his instruments heavy on his arms, but his heart as light as his stomach.

Berlioz was better than his word. Instead of "mentioning" the instruments of Sax, he devoted a good third of his *Journal des Debats* article to the extraordinary young inventor who had recently arrived in Paris.

"Named after its inventor, Monsieur Adolphe Sax from Brussels, the saxophone is a brass instrument with nineteen keys whose shape is rather similar to the ophicleide. The mouthpiece is similar to the bass clarinet. Thus the saxophone becomes the head of a new group, brass with reed. It has a compass of three octaves from . . ." And so on. The saxophone received a splendid introduction to Paris.

And Sax himself, when he kept his appointment to demonstrate his instruments at the Conservatoire, found that he, too, was being given an excellent introduction to the musical world of Paris. He was welcomed, praised, his demonstration appreciated and his instruments approved. The future looked bright.

A few days later it looked even brighter. People began to look him up, having read Berlioz's article or heard of the Conservatoire demonstration, and offered to invest money in the instrument factory he planned to build. Within a few days he had twelve thousand francs!

Sax rented a broken-down shed at No. 10 Rue Saint-Georges and started his factory. He bought tools and materials, trained a staff of workers, and soon was producing instruments.

Sax lost no opportunity to show his new saxophone to people of wealth and influence. Some of these people saw no good either in the instrument or its inventor; they called his pride arrogance and his self-confidence vanity. But others, like Berlioz, the composer Rossini, and General de Rumigny (aide-de-camp to the Emperor) welcomed the fine blend of sound the saxophone produced, and they recognized and admired the unusual combination of artist and mechanic in Adolphe Sax. Berlioz wrote another laudatory article about the inventor.

"A revolution is in the making," wrote Berlioz, "and Monsieur Adolphe Sax from Brussels, whose work we have just examined, contributes to it. A man of lucid brain, farseeing, tenacious, steadfast, and skilled beyond words, he is ever-prepared to replace workers incapable of understanding his projects or realizing them. Calculator, acoustician, and when required, a smelter, turner, and an embosser. He can think and act. He is the rare combination, one who both invents and accomplishes."

In addition to writing about Sax and his saxophone, Berlioz introduced them in concert. He re-wrote several parts of one of his own compositions for a concert of his own works to make a place for the saxophone. On the night of the concert, Sax, still improving his instrument, worked until the musicians went out on the stage, making some last-minute changes on his saxophone.

The publicity from the articles of Berlioz and the saxophone's debut in concert helped Sax to get more financial backing. Soon he had a genuine instrument factory and a flourishing business. Contrary to the custom of the Parisian instrument makers, Sax insisted on having every bit of the work done in his own factory, under his own eyes; he would not order parts from different factories, as did other makers, to be assembled in his shop.

Soon the Sax factory was making saxophones in various sizes. Before long he managed to introduce them into the French military bands. As his prosperity and his fame increased, the jealousy of other instrument makers grew, fanned by his own unfortunate ill-temper. In fact, Sax made so many enemies that they formed themselves into an organized society, with a president, a secretary, and a treasurer; they had branches in several other countries. The avowed purpose of the anti-Sax society was to discredit the inventor and secure all of his patents, which numbered over thirty by the middle of the nineteenth century. Various lawsuits were instituted, chiefly by Wieprecht of Berlin, whose own instruments competed with those of Sax. But the decision of the courts in every case favored Adolphe Sax. His enemies could make trouble among his workmen, dissipate his fortune with lawsuits, make life difficult and unhappy for him, but they could not rob him of his rightful glory as an inventor of genius.

In 1852 Charles Sax followed his son to Paris. With his father's help, Adolphe embarked on what was to be his greatest contribution to the world of music: he brought order out of chaos in wind-instruments.

Up to that time, French bands had been composed of a heterogeneous lot of instruments, all intent only on making as much noise as possible. There were keyed-bugles, ophicleides, cornets, Russian horns, of all sizes and descriptions. There was no relationship by groups, no uniformity of dimensions. There was a great deal of duplication of tone and color, and the valves of all the brasses were crude and ill-fitting; in fact, the valve was little more than the germ of an idea until Sax took it in hand.

Sax and his father undertook to reform the instruments of the band mechanically, as Wieprecht had previously reformed the Prussian bands from a musical or artistic standpoint.

After much investigation and experimentation to discover the proportions of wind instruments which would give the roundest, fullest tone, Sax renovated the best of the existing band instruments and threw out the poor ones. He used instruments of his own invention (notably the sax-horns and sax-trombas) to fill the gaps left by this wholesale discard.

When Adolphe Sax had finished his work, the French military band, instead of being made up of many unrelated instruments, was composed of several *families* of instruments, with a definite relationship, each with a specific place in the music of the band, and each one greatly improved mechanically, with smooth-working, dependable valves.

Although today the saxhorns and saxtrombas, which played such an important part in Sax's radical house-cleaning of the wind band, are seldom used in this country, the band is systematically organized in the way Adolphe Sax proposed, with soprano, alto, tenor, and bass in each family of instruments. His new hybrid instrument, the saxophone, perpetuates his name, but he did far more for the world than invent an instrument which is a link between the brasses and the woodwinds. He has often been called, with justice, the Father of the Brass Band.

PART THREE

Music from Horns

PRIMITIVE Man, who discovered the musical possibilities of the bow-string and the reed, eventually found another source of useful, if not pleasing, sounds.

One day he picked up the horn of an animal—a ram, a cow, a buffalo, or such. Perhaps he had found various uses for different-shaped horns, to carry arrows in, to drink from, to use as decorations.

This particular horn had a hole in the end; the tip had broken off. He started to throw the horn away; then he stopped. It would hold arrows just as well, even if there was a small hole at the end.

Something was caught inside the horn; a leaf or a bit of grass, probably. He tapped the horn against a tree to dislodge the obstruction, but without success. He tried to reach it with his fingers, but his hand was too big. Finally he put the broken tip to his mouth. The leaf tickled his lips and he blew, trying to dislodge the thing.

The result amazed him. A sudden raucous sound startled him so that he almost dropped the horn. Where had that noise come from?

Cautiously he raised the horn to his lips again and blew a

second time, duplicating his previous lip action. The same frightening blast shook the air. It came from inside the horn, caused by his own breath!

He had made a sensational discovery: animal horns could be more than mere receptacles or decorations. They could be used as signals for communication.

Much later, Primitive Man learned that horns could even make music. By varying his lip pressure, he could produce several different sounds—not all the sounds he might wish, by any means, but certain definite tones higher than the fundamental note of his horn. With horns of different length, these higher tones were different. He could not understand it, but he accepted it as one of the wonders of the horn.

We call these higher tones harmonics, and we understand nowadays the laws of tone production that make them possible:

(1) *When the column of air inside a horn is set in motion by the vibration of the lips, it produces a series of waves, which in turn produce sound.*

(2) *When the column of air vibrates as a whole, it produces the fundamental tone of the horn.*

(3) *By varying the pressure of the breath and lips, the air column can be made to vibrate in different ways: as a whole, in halves, in quarters, etc. The sounds produced by the fractional columns are called harmonics of the fundamental tone.*

(4) *The air column cannot be made to vibrate in any fraction desired, but only in certain fixed fractions.*

Primitive Man had taken the first step in the development of our modern brass instruments.

Harmonics on Wind Instruments

1. *The fundamental note.*

When the sound wave vibrates as a whole, the fundamental note of the instrument is sounded.

2. *The first harmonic, or octave.*

When the lips are tightened, and the instrument is blown harder, the vibration rate increases until the sound wave divides into two equal waves, giving a note an octave higher than (1).

3. *The second harmonic.*

When the lips are tightened still more and the instrument is blown still harder, the sound wave divides into three parts, giving a fifth higher than (2).

4. *The third harmonic.*

Even harder blowing and further tightening of lips divides the wave into fourths, giving a fourth higher than 3, or two octaves higher than 1. Many other harmonics are possible.

11. Upside Down and Backward

The shining big-belled French horn with its beautiful mellow tone bears little resemblance to the animal horn of the savage, but it is a direct descendant of that crude instrument.

Primitive Man soon discovered, as he had with pipe whistles and bow-strings, that the longer the horn, the deeper the tone that could be produced. As he advanced in experience and ingenuity, Man learned to make horns of metal, but still he copied the shape of animals' horns. (The Lur, an ancient bronze horn, was made in the exact shape of the tusk of a mammoth.)

Soon, however, he found that he could make horns of any length he wished; his horns were no longer restricted to the length of their natural growth on the heads of animals.

These horns were used for signals in the hunt. The very long tube (twelve to sixteen feet) necessary to produce deep tones, was extremely cumbersome. But metal can be bent, so the body of the horn was coiled into a circle to make it convenient to play and to carry. And it was carried proudly; the knights of old valued their horns, for the horn and the broadsword were the insignia of knighthood.

The modern French horn is unique in many ways:

It is the *most difficult* to play of any wind instrument, because of the great length and narrowness of its tube, and its small mouthpiece. Expert players use seven different kinds of lip efforts to get the tones they want.

It *blends* with different instruments better than any other brass, because of its sweet mellow tone.

It can give a *greater variety* of effects than any other wind instrument.

It is the only one of the brasses which is played with the *bell down.*

And it is the only instrument whose valves or keys are played with the *left hand* alone. And thereby hangs a tale.

In the 1750's Anton Joseph Hampel was a horn player in the famous Court Orchestra of the King of Poland in Dresden.

Like all horns of the time, the body of his horn was bent

into two complete circles of tubing. He had a number of crooks, or additional lengths of tubing, which deepened the tone; he could insert these at will, although, of course, it took a little time. As horn players had always done, Hampel held his instrument with the mouthpiece horizontal to his lips and the wide bell level with his head and pointing up. The tones he produced were harsh and brassy—but the horn's voice had always been like that. In fact, there had been (and still was) considerable opposition to the new practice of using the horn in the orchestra. Many people objected that its tone was far too coarse and vulgar to be used with the sweet and delicate violins and flutes.

But Hampel loved his horn. It was a real challenge to play an instrument like this, in which everything depended on the player. The flute and oboe had their tone-holes to shorten the column of air inside their tubes and change their pitch. The trombone had its slide which performed the same function. The violins could produce different notes by stopping the strings with the fingers. But the horn had only the lips of the player.

However, a horn player could produce a number of harmonics from the fundamental tone of his instrument. And, of course, the fundamental note could be changed by lengthening the horn's tube by inserting a crook (a coiled detachable tube) into the small end of the instrument. This changed the horn's fundamental and all its harmonics as well. In other words, a crook set the horn in a different key, but did not give the player any greater number of notes of the scale.

Hampel worked constantly to find better ways of getting desired notes from his instrument. He objected to the crooks;

they were a necessary evil, of course, but they often made the horn extremely difficult to blow. He particularly disliked the practice of inserting the crooks at the mouthpiece. This meant that each different-length crook caused the bell of the horn to be a different distance from the mouthpiece. It was most awkward and annoying.

So the horn-player figured out a new method of using crooks. He made interchangeable U-shaped tuning slides of varying lengths that could be inserted in the middle of the horn's hoop. He had J. Werner, instrument maker of Dresden, manufacture a horn like this for him in 1753.

The new horn, which Hampel called "Inventions-horn," satisfied him much better than the old instrument. The intonation was better, and besides, the horn was much more convenient to handle. But he did not stop looking for additional ways to improve his instrument.

About seven years later, Hampel hit upon a scheme which had a much more lasting effect on the horn than his tuning crooks.

The director of the Dresden orchestra, Johan Adolph Hasse, who enjoyed the tongue-twisting title of *"Königlich Polnischen und Kurfürst lich Sächsischen Kapellmeister,"* valued his reputation as an outstanding conductor and tried constantly to improve his orchestra.

One day in rehearsal he made his musicians go over and over a certain passage, trying to get the effect he wanted. But Hampel's horn was too loud to suit him.

"Pianissimo!" shouted Hasse. *"Pianissimo!"*

Hasse shouted at the horn player until he grew red in the face, but the horn was still too raucous.

During the next break, Hampel looked around desperately. He must find some way to soften the tone. Suddenly he noticed an oboist taking a wad of something out of the bell of his instrument, and he remembered that oboists often muffled the harshness of the contemporary oboe's tone with a wad of cotton or such.

"If the oboe can be muted by stuffing something into the bell," thought Hampel, "why can't the same thing be done with my horn?"

Quickly he leaned toward the oboist. "Do you have any more of that stuff?"

His fellow-musician handed him a ball of cotton wool, and Hampel hurried to try it out before the conductor should give the signal to resume rehearsal.

The other horn player, Carl Haudeck, looked at Hampel in amazement. "What in the world are you trying to do?"

"Trying to soften the tone for my solo passage that threatens to make Herr Hasse burst a blood vessel."

"You mean you think you're going to put a *mute* in your horn? As if it were an oboe?" Haudeck laughed incredulously. "An oboe is small; the player can easily reach the bell and mute it. But the horn . . . That's a different matter, my friend. You can't reach into the bell while you are playing."

That was true. With the bell of the horn level with his head and pointing up, Hampel could not reach into it to thrust in the mute. . . . Anyway, if he did manage to get it in, how on earth could he ever get it out in a hurry?

Hampel turned his beautiful shiny instrument over in his hands, looking at it thoughtfully as he considered the problem.

"I wonder," he said finally, "if I couldn't turn my horn over? Instead of holding it with the bell up, turn the bell down toward my lap. Then I could easily reach into it."

"You're crazy, man!" scoffed the other horn player. "If you reverse the horn, the mouthpiece won't be right. You'll never be able to blow properly."

The director was back at his harpsichord. (All conductors at that time worked from a harpsichord; the baton conductor had not yet appeared.) In a few seconds Hasse would call the orchestra to attention.

Quickly Hampel turned his horn to the new position and blew into it experimentally. The mouthpiece seemed odd at that angle, but he could manage a fair tone; although quite different from his usual tone, it was sweet and mellow.

With his right hand, Hampel thrust the borrowed cotton wool into the bell and blew again. To his amazement, the sound that emerged was not only still softer but it gradually dropped a semitone. It was a most unusual effect. Haudeck watched and listened, astounded.

The director rapped for attention, but Hampel had to test his new discovery again. He blew into the horn once more without the mute, and again with the wool stuffed inside; there was no doubt about it: the presence of an object in the bell lowered the pitch of the horn half a tone! The discovery was worth the scowl he received from Kapellmeister Hasse.

When the orchestra reached the horn's solo passage—the part that Hasse wanted pianissimo—Hampel thrust his mute into the bell of his horn and transposed at sight the music before him a half tone lower.

The conductor nodded at the horn player, beaming, as he

continued to play the harpsichord accompaniment. "That's it! That's it! Soft and beautiful. Perfect!"

When the rehearsal was over, Haudeck, too, experimented with the new technique. The two horn players discovered that the hand alone produced about the same effect as the cotton wool and was much easier to use, as well as being capable of dependable variations. Furthermore, Hampel learned that different methods of hand-stopping, combined with varied lip pressure, could *raise* the pitch instead of lower it.

It did not take long for Anton Hampel, experienced musician that he was, to realize that he had stumbled on a valuable technique in horn-playing. Although the hand-stopped notes were quite different in quality from open tones, by means of them the instrument was made almost chromatic, for many more notes of the scale were now possible. Moreover, the new playing position gave the horn tone a finer, sweeter quality. It was truly a revolutionary development.

Other horn players, quick to see the advantages of the new technique, took up the practice of hand-stopping. Soon composers began to indicate in their music that certain notes should be played with the hand in the bell.

Many years later the application of valves to the horn made hand-stopping unnecessary for obtaining chromatics. By pressing a valve, an additional length of tubing, permanently welded into the instrument, was brought into use. This instantly changed the fundamental note of the instrument.

But the practice of inserting the hand in the bell persisted because of the distinctive cooing quality it gave to the tone; hence, of necessity, the upside-down position carried on. And since the right hand, because of its greater dexterity, was used for stopping, when valves were added to the instrument the *left* hand was used to operate them.

Thus, instead of being *replaced* by the valve horn, the hand horn was really incorporated into the valve horn, and the so-called French horn (which is no more French than German or English) became the upside-down, left-handed instrument it is today.

12. Unsettled Controversy

If instruments were able to brag, the trumpet could undoubtedly out-boast the entire orchestra on the subject of genealogy. No other instrument has such a long and proud record of association with royalty and the highlights of history.

The trumpet dates almost from the beginning of civilization. It was used in the fall of Jericho, and in the Trojan War.

It was associated with wars and events which changed the destinies of nations and the map of the world.

For centuries the trumpet was the badge of royalty, and was used only in the king's service. Trumpeters had the standing of officers, and were allowed to wear the feather of nobility in their caps. The voice of the instrument, in keeping with its exalted position, was commanding and brilliant. And the trumpet was one of the first wind instruments to be accepted in the orchestra. Truly a proud record.

Although undoubtedly it started with a crude animal horn, the trumpet was very early made of metal. Gradually it grew longer and more slender. When it reached the length of four feet it was found to be unwieldy, and part of the tube was coiled to make the instrument a convenient carrying size.

With no valves or keys, it was impossible to play all the notes of the scale on one instrument. In fact, six notes (the fundamental and some of its harmonics) were about the limit of its repertoire. Naturally many men tried to remedy this defect. Hand-stopping was attempted, as with the horn, but the resulting muffled tones were so uncharacteristic of the noble trumpet's traditional voice that the experiment was abandoned.

Tone-holes and keys were tried, as on the oboe and the flute, but they were a sad failure; conical brass instruments did not respond to holes bored in them to shorten the air column as did the wood instruments.

Finally, removable crooks were applied to the trumpet, as on the "Inventions-horn" of Hampel, but changing the crooks was a nuisance. Moreover, it was extremely difficult for a player to master the problems of intonation in each crook.

Eventually a way was found to keep these crooks permanently attached, and direct air into them or away from them at will; and the discovery gave rise to a quarrel which has not yet been settled.

In 1816 Heinrich Stoelzel came to Berlin from Breslau, and was soon playing the horn in the Royal Kapelle in that city. His fellow band-members were amazed at his horn. Instead of adding crooks to change the key of his instrument, Stoelzel simply pushed down a piston which he called a valve. This, he claimed, acted just like a crook, adding another length of tubing to his horn and thus lowering the pitch.

"Where did you get that horn?" the other musicians asked.

"I made it," Stoelzel answered.

"But where did you get the idea for the valve?"

"I tell you I made this horn. I invented this valve myself. Experiment convinced me that the way to alter the pitch of a brass instrument is not by shortening holes, but by *extending* the compass as the trombone's slide does for that instrument."

"Why fool with anything to alter the pitch?" skeptical musicians asked. "Aren't crooks good enough for you?"

Stoelzel shook his head. "Crooks take time to change. Besides, it is hard to regulate the intonation, to change from one crook to another. Valves are much more certain."

A trumpet player laughed. "Yes, valves are certain—when they work. What if your valves get out of order? What will you do then?"

Others took up the argument. "That's right. Mechanical contrivances are prone to get out of order. It's far better to stick with the natural instruments. A good musician doesn't need any mechanical devices."

In spite of the skepticism of his fellow-orchestra members, however, Stoelzel was certain that his valve would eventually be adopted on all brass instruments. In order to safeguard the new invention, he secured a patent which would protect the tubular piston valve in Prussia for ten years. Then he persuaded the firm of Greissling and Schlott to make brass instruments, using the valve.

Accordingly a complete line of valved brasses—horns, trumpets, cornets, trombones, etc.—were built. But the new instruments were defective. The crude valves did not work as they were supposed to. Greissling and Schlott lost money. The opponents of the valve were quick to say, "I told you so."

How Valves Work

In principle, valves are like irrigating ditches with gates to shut them off or bring them into use at will.

A, B, and C are gates to their respective lengths of tubing. When all three gates are closed, air goes only between D and D', giving the fundamental note of the instrument.

When A is opened, that length of tubing (A to A') is added to D-D', giving a longer column of air, a longer wave length and consequently a deeper new fundamental note.

When A and B are both opened, both lengths of tubing are added, and so on. Seven combinations (seven different lengths of tube and consequent tones) are possible:

D only
D plus A
D plus B
D plus A and B
D plus A and C
D plus A, B, and C

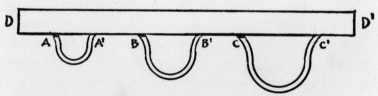

Stoelzel was disappointed, but not discouraged. He designed a new kind of valve. But it did not work, either. Then he went back to the tubular piston valve and tried to improve it.

About that time a Silesian bandsman, Frederick Bluhmel, arrived in Berlin. When he learned that Stoelzel claimed to have invented the piston valve, he was furious. "Why, I invented that valve myself," he cried. "I sold the invention to Stoelzel."

Stoelzel hotly denied Bluhmel's claims. "He is trying to take credit for my work. This idea is mine and it is patented. Let Bluhmel try to prove that it is his!"

Frederick Bluhmel produced some documents, but they did not satisfy the patent authorities of his prior claim. He swore he would make a better valve, one that would put Stoelzel out of business. And he proceeded to construct a valve that looked different but worked on the same principle as Stoelzel's piston-valve. Both valves were essentially a quick way of changing the crooks on a trumpet or a horn. The valve acted as a little tap which, when moved by a lever or a piston, directed wind into additional lengths of tubing which were welded into the body of the instrument.

Bluhmel's valve was good, but the king refused him a patent on the grounds that the field was already covered by Stoelzel's patent.

Bluhmel contested the case. For years the battle raged. All the musicians in Berlin argued the question among themselves. Some were opposed to valves on general principles; nothing, they said, could take the place of natural tones. Valves impaired the quality of tones. Valves were apt to stick or get out of repair. Far better to play well the notes your instrument could produce than to enlarge your repertoire but in so doing to become dependent on mechanical contrivances which might fail you.

Others were open-minded on the subject of valves. Some of these favored Stoelzel's claim; some favored Bluhmel's. And a few insisted that neither one was the real inventor of the valve. An Irishman named Charles Claggett, they said, had invented the basic idea of the piston valve many years before. So what was all the argument about?

By the time Stoelzel's patent had expired, the antagonism toward valves had begun to lessen. Instrument makers, not caring whether Stoelzel or Bluhmel or Claggett was really the inventor of the piston valve, began to use it on horns and trumpets. (A little later the rotary valve superseded the piston valve on the horn.)

In 1830 the valve system was improved by Müller of Mayence. Now three valves were used: one to lower the pitch a semitone, a second to lower it a tone, and a third to lower it a tone and a half. Now the trumpet was fully chromatic. Eventually Adolphe Sax perfected the valve, and the valved trumpet was here to stay.

Even after the valve was made practical, however, musicians did not readily take up the valved trumpet. The old crooks hung on for years. Gradually, however, the advantages of the valves were recognized and finally the valved trumpet came to be generally used (although the natural trumpet and the slide trumpet are still found occasionally). The valve really revolutionized the military band, and it made possible the purely brass band.

The old controversy about who invented the valve is still going on. But no trumpet player cares as long as the valves continue to give him, in the trumpet's clear, ringing voice, the chromatic tones he needs.

13. Son of a Serpent

Like the string section, which has four voices ranging from high to low (violin, viola, cello, and double bass), and the woodwinds with a comparable quartet (flute, oboe, clarinet and bassoon), the brass section also has a quartet of voices. Of these the trumpet is the highest; next comes the French horn; then the trombone; and deepest of all is the bass tuba.

The tuba is perhaps the least standardized of any instrument today. There are helicons, euphoniums, saxhorns, and sousaphones, which were made according to the suggestions of John Philip Sousa, the "March King," and named for him. Some of these instruments wind about the player's body, and some are held in the arms. Some have the bell forward, some have the bell back over the shoulder, and a few have the bell up. (Sousa specified that the sousaphone should "spread the music over the top of the band like frosting on a cake," but later the bell was turned forward.) Regardless of their differences, all of these instruments are members of the tuba family.

All tubas are made of metal. All have a huge bell, deep strong tones, and usually four valves to control the pitch. It is difficult to imagine anything less like a snake than a tuba, with its tremendous bell, its great conical tube, and its powerful voice. Yet the tuba descended from a serpent!

In 1824, at the age of twenty-two, Wilhelm Wieprecht left his post as violinist in the Gewandaus civic orchestra of Leipzig, and went to Berlin to play in the Royal Chapel orchestra there.

Although the symphony orchestra provided his livelihood, Wieprecht was keenly interested in band music. This was not surprising, for his father was a town musician of Aschensleben. Wieprecht had seen the pleasure music gave to the common people, who were never admitted to the symphony concerts played for royalty. The wind bands, which had grown from a merging of instruments used by town musicians and the trumpets and drums of armies, provided in their open-air concerts all the music the mass of the people would ever hear.

But what bothered Wieprecht, a sensitive, cultured musician, was that the band music was not *music*. It was noise. To put it bluntly, bedlam. The composition of bands and the way they were conducted pained Wieprecht's musical sensibilities. The symphony orchestra by now was fairly well standardized in make-up, with groups of strings, woodwinds, brasses and percussion; great composers had written for orchestra, and their works were produced with sensitivity and sympathetic interpretation. The military band, on the other hand, seemed interested only in making noise. The bandmaster seemed not to care whether his band was balanced as to tone, whether his instruments sounded well together, whether they produced the effect the composer wanted. Volume was what they aimed at—and got! Something should be done about it.

And something *could* be done about it. For one thing, the instruments could be vastly improved. Wieprecht was particularly intrigued by the possibilities of the valve system for brasses which had recently been introduced here in Berlin, and was still the center of a heated argument. Properly used, valves could revolutionize brass wind instruments, Wieprecht felt sure.

Yes, the wind band certainly had a future. The brasses had great potentialities with the lengthening-tube valve, and the woodwinds were rapidly being improved with their shortening-hole key system. Young Wieprecht wanted a hand in the future of wind bands. It promised to be interesting.

After several months of residence in Berlin, young Wieprecht found a chance to express his views to a military bandmaster. But the army officer was indignant. The idea of that young pup of a civilian violinist presuming to tell the Prussian army what to do! The bandmaster turned on his heel and walked off.

The cold reception his suggestions received annoyed young Wieprecht, but did not daunt him. At every opportunity, he urged the reorganization and reformation of bands. Before long bandmasters and band players crossed the street when they saw him coming, to avoid hearing his arguments again.

Then one day Wieprecht aired his views to the commanding officer of a German cavalry unit. The old soldier looked at the young musician quizzically.

"You're making quite a crusade of this band-reforming question, aren't you, young man? I've heard a lot about you lately."

Wieprecht flushed. He *had* talked an awful lot and antagonized many people.

"Y-yes, sir," he stammered. "But you see, it's important. Why, the brass band should be able to play good music just as well as the symphony orchestra. And it could, too, if . . ."

The officer held up his hand protestingly. "I know. If we would just improve the instruments, balance the band, and concentrate on artistic playing."

Wieprecht nodded eagerly. "That's it! That's it exactly, sir."

The commanding officer studied the eager young fellow. Ever since he had first heard about it from his irate bandmaster, he had been considering Wieprecht's suggestion.

"How would you like to take my cavalry band in hand and see what you can do with it?"

Wieprecht gulped. "Me, sir?"

"Yes, you!" barked the old soldier. "That is, if you really

know what you're talking about? Or are you just a fiddler who likes to hear himself talk?"

"Well, sir, I don't know *every* instrument, but I play clarinet, trumpet, trombone, and drums, although the violin is really my instrument. I've studied composition, and I've composed considerable music for . . ."

The army officer stopped the flow of words with a warning hand. "All right. All right. I've looked up your record. Report to me tomorrow morning and we'll work out the details."

With the backing of the sympathetic commanding officer, Wieprecht was able to put his theories into practice. He organized the cavalry band to include the following instruments:

2 high trumpets in B♭
2 key-bugles
2 alto trumpets
8 trumpets in E♭
2 tenor horns
1 bass horn
3 trombones

Except for the slide trombones, he insisted on all instruments being equipped with valves, in spite of the opposition he met from many of the musicians.

When he had organized the physical composition of the band to his liking, Wieprecht proceeded to direct them (and the bandmaster) in the proper use of their instruments. Each player must subordinate his music to the total effect, instead of playing, every man for himself, as loudly as he possibly could. He trained them in the performance of some of his own compositions for wind band.

After weeks of practice the band offered a sample of their new music in a concert before army officials. It was a great success. Why, it was real *music,* not just noise! The top officials were so delighted with the results of Wieprecht's work on the German cavalry band that soon he was asked to do the same thing for the bands of the Prussian Life Guards.

This was a big opportunity, indeed. Wieprecht threw himself into the work with all of his youthful enthusiasm and earnestness. He worked early and late, giving the members of those bands personal lessons to make sure they knew just how various compositions should be played. His experience with different instruments enabled him to teach with authority.

In spite of the magnitude of this task, it proved easier in some ways than his smaller job on the single cavalry band had been, for now that the bandmasters had seen the value of Wieprecht's ideas, he received more co-operation.

Just one thing bothered the youthful band expert. Most of the instruments available for his use were fairly good now, he thought. His trumpets had been modernized with piston valves, giving them full control of the chromatic scale. The horns had received similar help from the new rotary valve. The trombone with its slide was fully chromatic and capable of true tones.

But the basses! What confusion there was among the bass instruments! A more heterogeneous crew he had never seen than the bass instruments Berlin used in band, opera, and orchestra. "Serpents," most of them were called. And they were fully as ugly in appearance and in tone as reptiles. Invented near the end of the sixteenth century by a French churchman, the original serpent had been a wooden tube about eight feet long, covered with leather, and shaped in a grotesque series of zigzags so that it would not be unduly cumbersome, and also so that the player's fingers could reach and cover the small note-holes bored in the tube. This wooden instrument, which combined the shortening-hole system of the flute and the lip-reed method of sound-production common to brass instruments, had a coarse tone and its notes were habitually off-key.

In spite of these drawbacks, the serpent had multiplied. It was made in every possible size and key—all equally bad.

And now Wieprecht heard that another offspring of the serpent was making itself seen and heard in France. Called the ophicleide, or keyed serpent, it was made of metal in many sizes and pitches. It no longer had the zigzag reptile shape, but was bent up at the end into a bell. The pitch was changed by note-holes controlled by eleven keys.

The ophicleide was said to be a great improvement on the old serpent and was used in France in the opera and even in the symphony. But its tone was admittedly wild and barbaric, and its notes far from true; Wieprecht was sure that it could not be otherwise, for he was convinced that a lip-reed instrument, to have a clear, even, resonant tone, must use the full sounding length of its tube for every note of its scale. Shortening-hole keys could not be successful.

Yet he needed a bass instrument. The music the bands were performing had improved immeasurably since he had balanced the instruments and taught the bandmasters something about how music should be played. And he had transcribed much great symphonic music for band (eventually he transcribed most of Beethoven's symphonies). In all this music there were bass tones, too low for the trombones, which were necessary to fill out the harmony. What should he do about it?

Wieprecht finally decided that the solution might be a brass serpent (like the French ophicleide) but with valves instead of keys. Perhaps a change from the shortening-hole system of the serpent family to the lengthening-tube system of the trumpets and horns might improve the tone of the instrument. Certainly it was worth a try.

He went to the firm of Griessling and Schlott, instrument makers—the same firm that had made Stoelzel's first valve instruments. They agreed to try his suggestion of a valved ophicleide.

The first such instrument kept the ophicleide shape. It did not satisfy Wieprecht, but the tone was a sufficient improvement over the old serpent's to convince him he was on the right track.

By that time he had met a clever and competent craftsman, J. G. Moritz, who found Wieprecht's dream of a valved brass bass instrument challenging. Moritz offered to join Wieprecht on the project, and the two young men set to work in earnest, although the bandmaster could spare little time from his work with the Prussian Guards Bands.

By 1835 Wieprecht and Moritz had produced a bass instrument (still in the ophicliede form) which proved eminently satisfactory. It could reach to low E. It had five *Berliner-pumpen valves,*—a modification of existing valves—two operated by the left hand and three by the right hand; these rendered it completely chromatic. And its tones were incomparably more noble than those of the ophicleide, as well as much truer. At last Wieprecht had the bass instrument he needed for his bands.

And just in time, too. No sooner had he introduced his new instrument (later called the tuba after an old Roman instrument) into the bands than he was given the big opportunity of his life: he was appointed director-general of all the King's Guards Bands. Now he could put his theories into practice throughout all of Prussia.

Wilhelm Wieprecht did just that. He made Prussian military bands so homogeneous in make-up, so artistic in execution that they could—and did—play together in one vast concert. On May 12, 1838, in honor of the visiting Emperor Nicholas of Russia, Wieprecht conducted a memorable performance of sixteen infantry and sixteen cavalry bands, consisting of a thousand wind instruments and two hundred side-drummers!

In a few years' time the bands of Prussia became the model for bands throughout Germany and Austria, and eventually the envy of all Europe. The name of Wilhelm Wieprecht was honored as the father of the German wind band.

During their lifetime Wilhelm Wieprecht and Adolphe Sax carried on a bitter quarrel over their individual inventions and their contributions to the band; their respective claims were hotly defended by their friends. But the century which has intervened since their death has brought a new perspective. Today we see that each man made a distinct and valuable contribution: Adolphe Sax to the technical improvement of the instruments and their valves, and the systematic formation of instruments into families; Wilhelm Wieprecht to the artistic side of band-playing, reforming the instrumentation of the band, concentrating on tonal balance, and setting up the goal of good music well played.

And Wieprecht is also honored as the inventor of the bass of the windband, the tuba.

14. Rugged Individualist

If you could go back a hundred years and look in on an orchestra rehearsal in the middle of the nineteenth century (shortly before our War between the States), you would find comparatively little difference in the make-up of the orchestra or in the instruments themselves. The stringed instruments would look almost exactly as they do now, except for the violin's slightly longer neck and higher bridge. Woodwinds would look pretty much the same: flutes, oboes, bassoons and clarinets all with modern, or nearly modern, keymechanism. The brass section would surprise you only by the presence of unfamiliar instruments, especially basses that look like snakes; trumpets, horns, and trombones would show little difference. All in all, you would feel quite at home with the orchestra of the 1850's.

Go back another hundred years, to the middle of the eighteenth century (not long before our Revolutionary War). The orchestra of the 1750's is a different matter. There is no concert hall, no music-loving public. Concerts are given in palaces, under the patronage of wealthy princes; common people seldom get a chance to hear good music. The orchestra is very small. The string section has much the same members and still looks familiar, except that the bows are crude and stiff, and straight or slightly outcurved rather than incurved. The woodwinds are quite primitive: few keys, faulty intonation; it takes a genuine musician to make music out of any of them. The percussion section is almost lacking (only a drum or two) and the harpsichord amazes you with its omnipresence; instead of directing with a baton, the conductor sits at the harpsichord. The brasses show as much difference as any group; not a valve or a key in the whole lot; the French horns are played with the bell up, and their tone is harsh and brassy; there are many unfamiliar instruments, and various sizes of each kind. Only the trombone—although you would see it only in churches or in bands, not in orchestras—looks like an old friend.

Now go back still another hundred years, to the 1650's—shortly after the *Mayflower* landed in America. Now you scarcely know your way around at all. There is no organization, no uniformity. No two orchestras have the same combinations of instruments. And so many strange instruments!

Viols, lutes, lyres, clarions, flageolets, cornettos, and many others. A very few violins, small and weak-toned, an occasional flute which is a plain wooden tube with finger holes only, oboes called "hautbois" of a dozen different sizes, and natural trumpets (without valves). You would not see French horns in orchestra, in town band, or in the church, for they were used only in the chase as yet. Nor would you see trombones in the orchestra; aside from its use by town musicians in Germany, the trombone was employed only in the church, considered strictly an instrument for religious music. Of all the bewildering array of instruments you would see, only the trombone looks much like its modern counterpart.

And if you go back yet another hundred years, to the 1550's (half a century after the discovery of America), you would be utterly lost, musically speaking. No orchestra, no knowledge of harmony, very little instrumental group playing, and then only as accompaniment to singing. No printed music; not even *written* music as we know it today, for the measures were not marked off, and the whole score looked much like shorthand. And of all the primitive-looking and primitive-sounding instruments which you would find in church or palace or town band, the trombone alone would stand out as the only familiar one.

For at least four hundred years—and possibly a couple of centuries longer—the trombone, alone of all instruments, has remained substantially the same. How did it happen? Let Trombone tell his own story.

About the middle of the twentieth century, Trombone looked back on his long life with considerable satisfaction.

Other instruments liked to brag about their "progress" and hint that he had not progressed at all in five or six centuries. They didn't seem to realize that "change" and "progress" are not synonymous.

Trombone did not know how old he was. Some people thought he dated back to the hey-day of the Roman Empire. Others denied that, and insisted that the year 1300, roughly, was the date of his birth.

The time of his birth might be doubtful, but there was little doubt of Trombone's origin. Of a certainty the Trumpet was his father. Some unknown trumpet player, dissatisfied with his instrument, anxious to find a way to play more notes than the half-dozen harmonics his crude trumpet would produce, had discovered the slide principle. And there he—Trombone —was, full-grown. . . . Well, no; not exactly full-grown. It had taken many years of experimentation, of constant lengthening of his slide, before he reached his full chromatic growth.

But that was centuries ago. By 1520, before the days of the great Cremona violin makers of whom the string section loved to brag, Hans Menschel of Nuremberg, Germany, had become famous as a maker of fine trombones. His instruments differed little, if any, from Trombone, himself, today.

Of course, Trombone had not borne his present name at first. Often he was called a kind of Trumpet. Later he was termed Sackbut by the English (meaning "pump") and Pommer by the Germans. And—irony of fate—when people finally bestowed on him the name by which he was to be known for centuries to come, they chose Trombone, which means "big trumpet." Must he always be reminded of his relationship with his orchestra partner, that instrument of less-than-perfect intonations, the soprano of the brass family?

Time was, however, and not so many centuries ago, when Trombone had been proud to be seen in the company of Trumpet. That was in the days when Trumpet consorted with royalty, when only a noble-voiced instrument was deemed fit company for him. But even then, in spite of the opinion of kings and princes, Trombone had known himself to be far superior to Trumpet. For was not he—and had he not always been—fully chromatic? He alone, of all instruments save the strings, could form any wanted tone perfectly, providing his player was expert enough to set his slide in the right place and blow correctly.

Yes, Trombone had had a rich and full life. The medieval Church had depended on his voice to reinforce the plainsong of the chorus—a duty no other brass instrument could perform since none of them had control of all the notes of the scale.

From his early role in the Church, Trombone had progressed to royal and civic ceremonials, and to German town bands; then to opera and military bands; and finally, early in the nineteenth century he had made his sensational debut in the orchestra, in Beethoven's Fifth Symphony. . . . Actually, it had been a *re*-entry in place of a debut. Few people remembered that he had been a member of that history-making orchestra of Monteverdi's in 1607, but had subsequently been dropped from symphony favor, except for Handel.

How Trombone had suffered through his long life at the hands of players with insensitive ears or careless hands or inexpert lips! On the other hand, how he had gloried in his hours of triumph, manipulated accurately by players of real ability!

And it was so easy to play him, Trombone thought. For the life of him, he could not see why *anyone* couldn't do it well. His make-up was absurdly simple compared to Violin with his seventy different pieces, and Trumpet with his two hundred separate parts, and Clarinet with his intricate key-mechanism, and . . . Why, *all* the other instruments were far more complicated than he! Really, Trombone was nothing but two brass tubes with a U-shaped slide fitting over them, with a mouthpiece on the free end of one tube and a bell on the end of the other. Moving the slide out lengthened the air column inside his tubes, slowed down the rate of vibration, and consequently deepened his pitch. Moving it in shortened the air column, speeded up the vibration, and raised his pitch. What could be simpler?

Of course, Trombone had to admit, it takes practice and a true ear to learn just how far the slide has to be moved to obtain a certain note. Then, too, the correct use of the lips and breath takes time to master. The lips act as a vibrating reed, to set the air column in motion. By varying the tension of his lips or the pressure of his breath, the player can "over-blow" and obtain harmonics. Not easy, perhaps. But many players learned it. Why couldn't everyone? Why did his performance have to vary from excellent to horrible? Like the Violin, in the hands of a tyro, Trombone's voice was torture to listen to, while an expert could bring forth from the same instrument inspiring and heavenly music. Why such unfortunate extremes?

Doubtless some people felt that Trombone went to regrettable extremes in his choice of music to play as well as in his playing. Oh, he had noticed the lifted eyebrows and the muttered comments that greeted his recent interest in jazz. Highbrows thought he was betraying his noble tones, lending them to "hot licks." But Trombone himself did not feel that way about it. There are different kinds of music, just as there are different kinds of people. Who is to say which is better? And if his gift for glissando and wow-wowing adds immeasurably to jazz, why deprive that branch of music of his talents? After all, one must do what one can in the world; one must make the most of one's abilities.

That was what the other instruments who boasted about "progress" couldn't seem to understand: Trombone had to keep his own individuality. He had to hold onto and use the one characteristic which was truly his—the slide. (That poor relation of Trumpet, the Slide Trumpet, had a small slide, but really it acted only like a valve; it was not long enough to make the instrument truly chromatic, like Trombone.)

It hadn't been easy, all those centuries, resisting every effort to take his slide away from him, to change him into just another horn or trumpet. People had tried all sorts of things to make him over.

In the 1700's they had tried to dress him up by making his bell in imitation of a serpent's head! Trombone shuddered, remembering. . . . Fortunately, that dreadful device had impaired his tone and they gave it up.

Later, some general decided Trombone's bell should be turned backward, over the shoulder of his player, so that on the march the music would go back to the following army and the watching crowds. That didn't last long, either; Trombone could not remember why.

The next would-be improvements came thick and fast, a veritable epidemic of them. No sooner had Bluhmel and/or Stoelzel invented the piston valve than people tried to shove that down Trombone's throat—or rather, into his body. What a ridiculous scheme that was! Everybody knows that valves and keys are not accurate; they simply can't be, by the laws of acoustics. Then why put an imperfect tone-producing contrivance on an instrument that already has a perfect one? Ease of operation, they said. Bah! . . . Of course, the valve had persisted in some countries; his cousin, the Italian trombone, still used valves. But Trombone had his own opinion of such heretical nonsense.

Then the rotary valve came along, and men tried *that* on him, too. But with no more success, fortunately.

Trombone recalled the most outlandish of the attempts to harness him with valves. Adolphe Sax, the man who invented the saxophone and who standardized and perfected the brass section of the orchestra, thought he should apply a little of his ingenuity to Trombone. So he constructed a monster affair composed of six almost complete Trombones controlled by six shortening valves. The thing had seven huge bells! Imagine! Undoubtedly that man Sax was a genius, but even genius should know enough to let Trombone alone.

Trombone sighed, remembering. He hoped men had learned their lesson by now: never try to improve the perfect. . . . But probably they hadn't learned it yet; men were so stupid. Very likely he would have to spend the *next* five hundred years resisting so-called improvements, fighting to keep his own individuality, his complete integrity, his slide.

PART FOUR

Striking Music

LONG BEFORE he learned the musical possibilities of the hunting bow, reeds, and animals' horns, Prehistoric Man undoubtedly discovered instruments of percussion. He listened to stones falling from the mountainside; when they fell on soft earth or on logs the sound was dead and dull, but when they crashed against other rocks the sound was sharp, clear, and resounding. Man found that he could clap two stones together and make a satisfying noise.

Sticks made a different sound, he discovered. As he threw logs on his pile of firewood, he listened to the clatter and noticed that the impact of wood against wood made a distinctive sound, unlike that of stone against stone. He had found another noise-maker.

One day after a storm which uprooted many trees, he noticed that most fallen logs gave very little sound when tapped, while certain others gave off a hollow, resonant tone. Investigation proved that a hollow log made an excellent noise-producing instrument—the loudest one he had yet found.

Later on, when Man learned to stretch and cure the skins of animals for various uses in his shelter, clothing, and weapons, he made another interesting discovery: the tautly stretched skin of an animal vibrates when struck, making a thin, hollow sound.

Prehistoric Man now had all the necessary ingredients for percussion—music made by hitting or striking.

The percussion section has often been called, with reason, the "stepchild of the orchestra." The string section is, of course, the eldest son, since the orchestra began with the strings and grew around them. The second son is the woodwind section, for the oboe and bassoon were taken into the orchestra almost at the beginning. The brass section is an adopted son, since its members were taken over from the army (trumpets), the hunt (horns), and the church (trombones).

Each of these three sons has a stable and accepted place in the orchestra family. Each of these groups has a leader. Each knows the part it is expected to play in the ensemble.

On the other hand, the percussion section never knows where it stands. Sometimes it is overworked. More often it is neglected, almost forgotten. Where each member of the other groups has only one instrument to play, or two at the most (flute and piccolo, clarinet and bass clarinet, oboe and English horn, bassoon and double-bassoon), the poor percussion player must be ready at a signal to play any one of a dozen different instruments, and frequently two at a time. Sometimes he must sit idly by for hours, yet be expected to come in promptly and accurately with a single "clang" or "boom."

The percussionist must be patient, alert and agile; he must have quick fingers, a sensitive ear, and an excellent sense of rhythm.

No Tune At All

Most of the instruments of percussion have no definite pitch. They are strictly for accent and rhythm, and for dramatic effect.

Although practically all of our modern instruments of percussion evolved from Prehistoric Man's experiences and observations, different instruments developed further in different countries.

The cymbals, a pair of hollowed-out brass plates which give a powerful crashing effect when properly struck together, came from Turkey; the best ones are still made in that country, but they are now used all over the world.

The gong, or tam-tam, came from China. It is a huge circular plate of hammered metal which gives a low, mysterious tone.

The triangle came from the Orient, probably from Turkey. It is a round metal bar shaped into a nearly closed triangle, hung by a gut string and struck with a metal beater. It gives a clean bell-like tone.

Castanets, nowadays, are associated with Spanish music, but they were probably introduced into Spain by the Moors. Made in pairs of hollow pieces of hard wood or ebonite, castanets are clicked together by the fingers or fastened to a handle and shaken. They produce a dry, clicking sound which is particularly adapted to syncopation.

Like the castanets, the tambourine is considered Spanish,

but it was known in ancient Egypt, Assyria, and Greece. It is really a small drum with only one head. Calfskin is stretched tightly over a round wooden frame; small metal discs, in pairs, are inserted in the frame at intervals. The tambourine makes several different sounds, depending on whether it is struck with the hand, shaken, or the drum head rubbed with the thumb.

The tambourine is only one type of drum. There are as many other kinds as there are countries and races of people, for every land, every society has had its drums, from the signal drums of the African jungle to the ceremonial drums of the American Indians to the huge bass drum of the modern army band on parade. The drum is a universal instrument. The day that Man first put together his two best noise-makers, the hollow log and the taut animal skin, marked the real beginning of the best of all percussion instruments: the drum.

15. Brotherhood of Drummers

If you have never held a pair of drumsticks in your hand, you are apt to be one of those people who believe that there is nothing to drumming—that anyone who can keep time can beat a drum. If, on the other hand, you have had some experience with drums, you know that drumming is as much an art as violin playing. In fact, men who have spent a lifetime at the drums say they are continually practising and improving their technique.

Music is made up of rhythm, melody, and harmony. Of these, rhythm is perhaps the most important. If you don't believe it, try this: play "Jingle Bells," giving each note the same value; then tap out the rhythm of the song without any tune; and see which is the more characteristic of "Jingle Bells," the more easily recognized.

The drum is the chief instrument of rhythm, and the snare drum (or side drum) is the most popular of all drums in America. A descendant of Primitive Man's log drum, the side drum was a soldier's instrument almost from its beginning. For several hundred years it remained strictly a military property. Gradually it made its way into town bands, and into the symphony orchestra, but its heart remained in the army.

Naturally, then, the history of the snare drum and drumming is closely related to the history of wars and soldiers. Yet the man who contributed a great deal to the improvement of all kinds of drums in this country, and who initiated an organization destined to help make American military drumming the envy of the world—that man was never a soldier at all.

In September of 1933, the American Legion Convention was being held in Chicago. Men who had served in the United States armed forces during World War I were gathered from all parts of the country. Old "buddies" were reunited. Reminiscences and anecdotes were recounted over again. Battles were re-fought in retrospect.

One non-veteran in Chicago was intensely interested in this American Legion convention. He was William F. Ludwig, head of the WFL Drum Company in Chicago, which he had founded more than twenty years before with the help of other members of his family. His company had made the first successful pedal timpani manufactured in this country, and had contributed many improvements to drums and accessories for band and orchestra.

But William Ludwig was interested in more than merely making drums. From the time when, as a child of eight, he had announced his intention of becoming a drummer, Ludwig had never lost his love of drum-playing. Even the three long years he had had to study with drumsticks and pad alone, before he was allowed to use a drum, did not discourage him. During the forty-odd years which had intervened since, he had held almost every conceivable type of position open to a drummer: in ice-skating rinks, dance bands, minstrel shows, circus bands; in theater and vaudeville orchestras, symphony orchestras, grand opera. Yes, Ludwig had been nearly every kind of a drummer—except a military drummer.

And he had even had a sort of second-hand experience with that. For years he had been teaching various drum corps which the American Legion had formed. This accounted for part of his interest in the Legion convention which was here in Chicago now.

But Ludwig's interest was based on more than a desire to see fellow-drummers of the American Legion. An idea had been brewing in his mind for some time. This was the opportune moment to see if it would work.

Bill Ludwig went to the convention hall at the close of the afternoon session. In a short time he had rounded up a dozen of the best drummers of the country.

"What's up, Bill?" one of them asked. "What's the idea?"

"Come on with me," Ludwig answered. "A bunch of the boys are going to show what they can do on the drum."

So "a bunch of the boys" gathered in the Lyon and Healy building. There was George Lawrence Stone, drum instructor of Boston; Harry Thompson, arranger and composer of special drum corps music; George A. Robertson, of Chicago; Bill Flowers, active in the Legion's state and national drummer contests; Bill Kieffer, drummer with the United States Marine Band; Bill Hammond, of Pittsburgh; Joe Hathaway, the Legion's national champion drummer of the previous year; Roy Knapp, studio drummer of radio station WLS; Heinie Gerlach, four times national champion drummer of the American Legion; Billy Miller, prominent drummer of Chicago; Edward B. Straight, author of many drum books; and last but not least, J. Burns Moore, dean of Connecticut drummers.

And they did, indeed, show what they could do on the drum. For hours, rolls, flams, drags, paradiddles echoed through the halls, as the thirteen experts vied with each other in drum performance.

While the fun was at its height (some six or seven hours later) Bill Ludwig aired his idea.

"You fellows are a pretty representative group of the best drummers in America," he said.

"Don't forget yourself, Bill," someone put in. "You fit that category pretty well still."

Bill Ludwig smiled and went on. "We all know the basic rudiments of drum playing . . . long roll . . . five-stroke roll . . . seven-stroke roll. . . ."

Twelve voices took it up, though not in the same order.

"Nine-stroke roll." "Drag." "Ruff." "Ratamacue." "Paradiddle." "Eleven-stroke roll." "Double-drag."

Ludwig interrupted, laughing. "Okay, okay. We all *know* them. But we don't all *do them alike.* Some of us, especially those of us here in the Middle West, were raised on the Bruce and Emmett manual of drum playing." Robertson, Knapp, and Miller nodded. "But others—you fellows from New England, for instance—swear by Strube's method." Stone, Moore, and Hammond nodded in their turn. "In other words, there isn't enough uniformity in drum-playing."

"You're right, Bill," agreed Kieffer of the Marine Band. "One drummer executes a roll finishing with the right hand, and another does it finishing with the left."

"But what can we do about it?" asked Hathaway. "We all play the way we were taught."

"Well . . ." Ludwig paused impressively and looked around at the other men. "If we formed an association of drummers and set up regulations and standards . . ."

George Lawrence Stone got the idea immediately. "Why, sure! In time an association like that would standardize drumming technique all over the country—bands, orchestras, schools—just as the adoption of Strube's manual by the Army standardized military drumming after the War between the States."

One of the men shook his head. "It wouldn't work. We'd never agree. The Strube men would insist on Strube technique, and the Bruce men would hold out for *his* method."

"And what about all the other drum methods on the market?" objected another. "Not everybody uses Strube or Bruce."

J. Burns Moore, from Connecticut, spoke up. He was older than most of the men, and his reputation as a drummer was unassailable. "We would have to arbitrate. Surely, in the interests of a cause like this, which would bind all drummers into a firm fraternity, we could each afford to give up some pet bit of technique."

Twelve heads nodded soberly.

Ludwig was quick to take advantage of the temporary agreement. "Why don't we form our organization right now? I nominate Burnsie for president."

By the time the meeting broke up (at 4:30 A. M.) the National Association of Rudimental Drummers (or N.A.R.D. as it is popularly called) was duly formed, with J. Burns Moore as president, George Lawrence Stone as vice-president, and William Ludwig as secretary. Before many months had passed, the association had taken in several hundred members, and had adopted a set of twenty-six rudiments which would be standard. Each member pledged himself to widen the scope and influence of the association by encouraging drummers from all varieties of bands and orchestras to qualify for membership. (The only qualification was—and is—the ability to play the thirteen required rudiments of the twenty-six, to the satisfaction of any member of N.A.R.D.) They insisted that these rudiments are a sound basis for any type of drumming.

As the years have passed, N.A.R.D. has grown, and with it uniformity in drum corps. During World War II, the performance of American drum corps drew praise from many other countries, thanks in large part to the standardization of drum technique which N.A.R.D. had sponsored.

So snare drum technique became of age. And while old-timers still love to argue the relative merits of the Strube and the Bruce-Emmett systems, all support the compromise rudiments worked out by N.A.R.D. for the sake of a strong brotherhood of drummers.

In Tune

Each percussion instrument has its own distinctive sound and tone-color, but most of them have no definite pitch. Regardless of the key signature of the music being played, bass drum, snare drum, tambourine, triangle, cymbals, gong, castanets, and wood blocks make their own particular sounds, the same pitch each time.

To most people the word "percussion" means noise. To some it means rhythm. Relatively few people realize that some instruments of percussion can produce not only accent and rhythm but definite tune as well.

16. Quick Fingers and Keen Ears

The timpani, or kettledrums, are by far the most important of the instruments of percussion. (The phrase "the drums" is often used to designate the timpani.) And they are the only drums that have definite pitch.

Today a kettledrum consists of a huge rounded bowl of copper, brass, or silver over which is stretched a vellum drumhead which can be tightened to raise the pitch or loosened to lower it. The hollow bowl acts as a resonating chamber and considerably improves the tone. Kettledrums are usually played in pairs; sometimes three or more are used, but never one alone.

The kettledrums came from the Orient, probably from Arabia. Originally they were made of half-gourds covered with skin, and were small enough to be held in one hand and played with the other. They always accompanied the armies to war.

When metal began to be used in kettledrum manufacture, they were made larger and larger. Naturally, the bigger they grew, the harder they were to carry; so they were strapped to the player's waist, one on each side. They continued to ride to battle as of old. It was in this form that they were introduced into Europe after the Crusades. They were regarded as royal instruments, to be used in the exclusive service of kings and princes, usually in war; no one below the rank of Baron was permitted to own them.

When kettledrums reached the magnitude of our present-day timpani, it became impossible for a player to carry them around. By that time, however, the transportation problem did not matter, for the kettledrums had dropped out of the army. They had found their place in the orchestra, and they left military matters to their more portable brothers, the side drum and the bass drum.

For about two hundred years the place of the timpani in the orchestra proved very small and unimportant and monotonous. It was not until a deaf composer, unhampered by actual sounds, wrote music which he heard only in his imagination, and a young drummer took his job of playing seriously, that the kettledrums came into their rightful place as valuable tonal members of the orchestra.

When Felix Mendelssohn, composer and conductor, went to Leipzig in 1835 to take charge of the Gewandaus (a permanent orchestra supported by the music-loving people of the German city), he was not content to direct the same music the orchestra had been playing for years. Much great music had been written recently; much was still being written; and there were many wonderful pieces of old masters, particularly J. S. Bach, which had never been heard in Leipzig. So Mendelssohn, in his genial, happy way, persuaded his orchestra to add one new composition after another to their repertoire.

All went well until they tackled Beethoven's *Emperor Concerto*. This piece by the greatest of living composers (who, though he had lost his hearing, continued to write music) had a solo for timpani near the end. To Mendelssohn that solo was important; if it were not well done, the whole finale suffered. And the timpanist of the Gewandaus simply could not play it right.

Really, it was no reflection on the timpanist. After all, kettledrums were not supposed to play solos. For centuries they had been used with the trumpets in fanfares and calls to battle. After they entered the orchestra, in the seventeenth century, kettledrums and trumpets continued to be paired off. Composers never thought of giving the timpani a solo to play—until this radical fellow Beethoven came along.

People said that Beethoven was deaf. Perhaps that explained why he had the audacity to write such an outlandish thing as a solo for kettledrums. If he could hear his music, he would know how preposterous it was; the timpanist was sure of that.

When Mendelssohn saw that his timpani player could not handle the kettledrum solo, he looked around immediately for someone to take his place. But kettledrummers were hard to find. In fact, the post of kettledrummer was usually given to a player who was too old or too feeble to continue in any other instrument; and the conductor of the Gewandaus knew that feebleness and senility were two attributes he did not want in a new timpanist.

At last someone referred Mendelssohn to a young theological student at the university, Ernst Gotthold Pfundt by name, who was also chorusmaster at the Leipzig theater. Although a singing divinity student did not sound like a very good prospect, Mendelssohn looked him up.

"You are Herr Pfundt?" he asked.

"Ernst Gotthold Benjamin Pfundt. At your service."

Mendelssohn bowed courteously. "I was told you might be able to handle the post of timpanist in the Gewandaus orchestra."

Pfundt frowned. "Timpanist? That isn't much of a job, is it?"

Mendelssohn studied the young man doubtfully. "Have you had any experience in an orchestra?"

"Well—no. Not exactly. But I've played some in small ensembles, with my uncle and some friends."

"What instrument do you play?"

"The piano." Mendelssohn's hopes fell. But Pfundt went on quickly, "That is, the piano is the only one I'm really at all proficient on. But when I was a child I learned to play various wind instruments."

The conductor's hopes remained at a low ebb. He did not need any more clarinets or horns.

"I learned to play the drums, too," Pfundt finished brightly.

Mendelssohn's face cleared. "Kettledrums?"

"Oh, yes. Kettledrums, too."

Silence fell. Finally Mendelssohn broke it. "There's a solo for kettledrums in this composition we're working on now, Beethoven's *Emperor Concerto*."

Pfundt's eyes gleamed. "A solo? For kettledrums? I never heard of such a thing."

"The solo is very important. It is short, but must be done just right. It requires someone with very skilful and agile fingers who can re-tune his instrument rapidly. And, of course, it requires a keen ear and a perfect sense of rhythm."

Pfundt was definitely interested now. "There might be a future in that job, after all. How much is the salary?"

By the time the interview ended, the young theological student had agreed to give the timpani post a trial.

Mendelssohn left, shaking his head ruefully. The young fellow acted as if it were the Gewandaus and its director that would be on trial, instead of Pfundt himself.

Ernst Pfundt reported to the Gewandaus for a trial. And Mendelssohn was surprised and delighted with his performance. Pfundt brought to the kettledrums not only the two chief essentials of a good timpanist: accurate sense of pitch and excellent rhythm; in addition, he brought to his work boundless enthusiasm and a willingness to try anything.

With Pfundt at the timpani, Beethoven's *Emperor Con-*

certo went so well that Mendelssohn was encouraged to try other new works with radical innovations in the timpani part. And Pfundt was equal to all of them. He could change the pitch of his drums quickly and accurately during the course of a composition, although it meant tightening or loosening ten to twelve screws on each kettle, and determining the right pitch by ear with a storm of rival tones battering against him from all sides. Under Pfundt's skilful hands the kettledrums became instruments of rich tone and amazing agility, and the fame of Mendelssohn's timpanist spread far and wide.

But Pfundt worried about the difficulty of tuning his drums. Suppose his fingers should lose their dexterity? How, then, would he be able to change the tuning in the midst of a composition? There should be some quicker way of altering the tension of the drumheads. Couldn't some mechanism be worked out?

After that, each time he manipulated the screws, Pfundt considered ways and means of doing it mechanically. Eventually he worked out a foot pedal which connected with all of the screws and tightened or loosened them at will; he called it the *Maschinenpauke*. It was a crude and clumsy apparatus to operate, made of heavy iron forgings, but it gave much quicker results than hand tuning.

Pfundt was jubilant. Now the timpani could hold its own with other instruments. With his invention the timpani, like the violin and the trombone, could play a true glissando. Pfundt felt that he had really accomplished something worthwhile for his beloved kettledrums.

And so he had. But the pedal-tuning apparatus was the least of it; that had been tried before his time, and would be improved time and again after his death. Pfundt's greatest contribution to timpani playing lay in his attitude toward it: to him kettledrum playing was an art, to be taken seriously and mastered, like that of any other instrument. He gave timpani playing a dignity and an importance it had never had before. Pfundt set the standard for all timpanists who have followed him.

Just as Beethoven, in his compositions, showed what the kettledrums could be made to do, Ernst Pfundt showed how to make them do it. And the kettledrums were able to establish the place they hold today as the most important of all percussion instruments.

17. Straw-Fiddle's Descendant

The giant carillon at Riverside Church, New York, and the lyre-shaped glockenspiel carried in the high school band seem to have little in common. Yet they are brothers.

Early composers could not use the sound of bells in their music because carillons were too large to be transported and too expensive to be installed in a concert hall. Then someone discovered that metal tubes would almost duplicate the sound of bells, yet take up far less space. Finally it was learned that metal bars were even better and more compact. Furthermore they lacked the overtones which in true bells, often produce discords. Thus the so-called orchestra bells came into being: a series of flat metal bars tuned to the scale and arranged on a frame. This instrument is a tiny brother of the giant cathedral carrillon and gives a satisfactory reproduction of its tones.

Of all groups of instruments, the bell family includes the greatest variety of materials and forms and methods of playing: metal bars, wooden bars, metal tubes; bars struck in the center with hammers, tubes struck on the end; hammers wielded by hand, and hammers operated by keyboard. Glockenspiel, chimes, xylophone, marimba, vibraphone, and celesta—all belong to the bell family. All are members of the percussion section of the orchestra. All are instruments of definite musical pitch. And all evolved from Primitive Man's observations of the distinctive sounds of falling stones, clattering sticks, rattling pebbles and dry gourds.

The bell family is very old, and like the drums, it encircles the world. Little is known about the development of most of its instruments, but the origin of one of the youngest can be traced quite accurately.

In 1844 Victor Mustel, a French carpenter, made a momentous decision. He would change occupations. He would sell his ship-building business in Sanvio and go to Paris to become an instrument maker.

For a man nearly thirty years old, with a wife and two children to support, this was indeed a daring decision. His long apprenticeship in carpentering, his years of experience in ship-building—all would go for nothing except the skill they had given him in the use of tools. And what if he should not be successful in the new trade? What if the competition in the big city should prove too much for one who had lived all his life in a small town? What would happen to his family?

Mustel knew the chance he was taking, but he seemed driven by an irresistible urge. Ever since he had begun to experiment with that accordion he had bought in Havre (trying first to repair it, and later to improve it) he had known that building musical instruments, not boats, was his mission in life.

So the modest business in Sanvio was disposed of for a meagre price and the Mustel family moved to Paris in May of 1844.

For nine years Victor Mustel worked in different factories, earning little but learning much. Somehow he managed to feed and clothe his family (though not well) until at last he was made foreman in Alexandre's harmonium factory at a fair salary.

A few months later, in 1853, Mustel made another courageous decision. He would open his own factory. With no assets but unceasing energy, boundless confidence, and constructive genius, he founded the harmonium firm of "Victor Mustel." As might have been expected, since he had no money reserve and no influential friends to back him, the first few years were lean ones. Orders came in so infrequently that Mustel often had weeks with no work to do.

But he could not bear idleness, so he spent his time trying to improve the harmonium, or melodeon as it was sometimes called. The result of these voluntary labors was a new harmonium with two note-worthy improvements: knee pedals for controlling the volume (called "double expression") and a new stop which he called *harpe eolienne*. This improved instrument, exhibited at the Paris Exhibition of 1855, won a first prize. Mustel felt greatly encouraged and believed that his luck had changed.

At first it seemed that his optimism was justified. The interest aroused by the publicity given his prize brought business to the struggling firm. Fortunately Mustel's sons were now old enough to be of some help, and he was able to execute his commissions promptly and efficiently.

Then, unaccountably, business declined. Income scarcely equalled outgo. The family was kept from starving only by the sale of a little land inherited from Mustel's father. The 1860's were long, hungry years. Again Mustel had unwelcome leisure. And now it was even more important than ever that he keep busy, for he must train his sons in his craft.

Again Mustel turned to experimentation. This time it was the development of a new instrument that engaged his attention. The tuning fork which had been invented nearly a century previous by John Shore, trumpeter to George I of England, and an "ever tuned organ" patented by the Irishman Charles Claggett, inspired Mustel to construct an instrument which he called *Le Typophone*. It consisted of a number of graduated tuning forks in a resonator box; tones were produced by striking the tuning forks with hammers.

The typophone, completed in 1865, did little to improve the financial situation of the firm, which was now known as "V. Mustel and Sons." There was little demand for his new instrument. But it proved to be the basis, many years later, for an instrument which was to bring fame to Victor Mustel.

After thirteen years of struggle, Mustel's industry and perseverance won out. Business began to come his way. The fine careful workmanship of Mustel and his sons received its rightful recognition at last. The firm of "V. Mustel and Sons" became known as expert harmonium makers. Their instruments were noted for precision and fine finish. Eventually they had all the work they could handle. After a lifetime of poverty, the sons knew prosperity at last.

As the years passed (short, busy years now) Victor Mustel continued to work at experimentation and invention, even though his flourishing business necessarily absorbed most of his time. Various improvements for the harmonium, a new type of melodeon known as the "Mustel organ," and a different instrument which he called *le metaphone*—all these added to his fame but failed to satisfy the urge which had originally driven him to give up a secure income for an uncertain occupation: the urge to build and improve musical instruments.

Victor Mustel was past seventy when he built the instrument on which his fame rests, the celesta.

"Colorism" was now the keynote of symphonic music. New effects, startling tone colors were wanted. Due to this tendency, the percussion section of the orchestra was coming into its own at last, and was growing by leaps and bounds. From a pair of kettledrums which for centuries had been practically the only accepted instruments in this group, the percussions now employed bass drum, snare drum, tubular bells, castanets, rattles, triangles, and xylophone, as well as wood blocks, whistles, etc. Still composers continued to seek new and different instruments for special effects.

The xylophone particularly interested Mustel. Originally called "straw-fiddle" in its native Tyrol because it then consisted merely of wooden bars laid in a bed of straw, the instrument had become known as xylophone or "sounding wood." Now it was a series of rosewood bars on stretched cords in a frame, played with small hammers held in the hand. Saint-Saens had introduced it into the orchestra in 1874 in his *Danse Macabre*.

The xylophone's hard, hollow tone was brilliant, but of short duration. Mustel wondered if it were possible to sustain the tones in some way.

His thoughts carried him back to his own invention of twenty years previous, his typophone. He began to experiment with that little tuning-fork instrument.

After a great deal of work and research, the celesta took shape. It was a combination of half a dozen percussion instruments. Like the orchestra bells, it had graduated bars of steel, whose pitch was in direct proportion to their thickness, and in reverse ratio to the square of their length. Like the xylophone, the bars were set in vibration by hammers. Like the pianoforte, the hammers were put into action by keys. An accurately tuned resonator of wood was placed under each metal bar to enrich and prolong the tone. In addition, there was a pedal to increase sustaining power. The whole instrument, with a compass of five octaves, looked like a small upright piano and was played like one. Its tone, however, had a character all its own, sweet and delicate and fairy-like: "celestial."

Patented in 1886, the celesta created only mild interest in

orchestral circles for several years. Then one day in 1891, the Russian composer Tchaikowsky happened to visit Mustel's workshop in Paris. In the course of his stay the composer noticed what seemed to be a miniature piano.

"What is that?" he asked.

"A celesta," answered Mustel. "My latest invention." The instrument maker, now an old man, demonstrated the little instrument.

Tchaikowsky was delighted. He took Mustel's place at the keyboard and amused himself with improvising fanciful melodies on it.

"It is the very thing I need," he cried at last. "The delicacy . . . the sweetness of tone . . . these I shall make use of. I shall write a piece for the celesta."

And he did. For his *Nutcracker Suite*, which he was working on at the time, Tchaikowsky wrote "The Dance of the Sugar Plum Fairy," giving the celesta a solo spot.

When Tchaikowsky's *Nutcracker Suite* was presented in concert for the first time, Mustel's celesta made its debut, also. It was so successful that this ethereal-voiced descendant of the old straw-fiddle made a permanent place for itself among the percussion instruments of the orchestra.

PART FIVE

Music from Keys

ΙT TOOK Prehistoric Man only a few centuries to discover the basic principles of stringed instruments, pipes, horns, and percussion instruments.

Several thousand years then passed before another group of instruments—the keyboard family—came into existence. Once developed, however, keyboard instruments took the lead over all others. For centuries they ruled the world of music, until the symphony orchestra, which one of the keyboard instruments (the harpsichord) sponsored, eventually freed the other instruments from the domination of the keyboard family.

18. When Playing Was Work

Did you ever make a "shepherd's pipe"? It is a simple instrument, sometimes called "pipes of Pan," consisting of several graduated reeds (or soda straws) fastened side by side, on which you can make the notes of the scale with your breath.

If you have ever constructed one of these crude instruments, you have made an organ, for the huge church organ of ten thousand pipes is merely an elaboration of the "pipes of Pan." An organ is fundamentally a big box of whistles.

Although the organ is the father of all keyboard instruments, for the first thousand years of its existence it had no keys at all. Instead, it was a wind instrument, pure and simple. (It is still a wind instrument, of course, as well as a keyboard instrument.)

The history of the organ is long, complex and fascinating. Only one facet of it can be traced here. The earliest organ was probably similar to your "shepherd's pipe": a row of perhaps eight reeds, of unequal length and thickness, fastened together with wax. Like yours, it was played by blowing across the ends of the reeds.

Later the pipes were inserted into a small air chest, to which air was supplied by mouth through a tube. The fingers were used to close the tops of the pipes whose sound was not wanted.

As more pipes were added for additional notes and greater volume, it became impossible for ten fingers to cover all unwanted pipes, and equally impossible for a single pair of lungs to provide the necessary wind. Mechanized substitutes for fingers and lungs had to be devised.

In place of fingers, slider valves were made to open and close the lower ends of the pipes. In place of lungs, bellows were added to supply the air. Each slide had to be opened by hand to allow that pipe to speak, and it had to be closed again before another pipe was opened, to prevent the discord of two pipes speaking at once. Only one note was played at a time; harmony was still unknown.

It took several men to work even a moderate-sized organ: two or more to manipulate the valves and four or five—perhaps even a dozen—to operate the bellows. In one of the best

Medieval organs, the bellows were pumped in this fashion: each man ran up a little staircase and then jumped down on the bellows to force the air out of them. Then while the bellows were being raised by a system of pulleys, the man ran up the staircase again ready to jump on the bellows once more. For every note produced by the organ tremendous energy had to be expended.

Before long some genius added levers to the sliders which opened and closed the pipes. Each lever was labeled with a letter of the alphabet to designate the relative tone that particular pipe produced. Now a single man could "play" the organ, providing the bellows-blowers kept the instrument supplied with wind. When the organist pushed down a lever, the valve opened, allowing air to enter the pipe and produce a tone. When he released the lever, the valve would close, due to the action of a stiff spring.

After the introduction of levers, it was only a step to making a key out of a lever by fastening a platform on its end. These first keys, which were added to the organ about the tenth century, bore little resemblance to modern organ keys. They were about five or six inches wide, a yard or more long, and had to be pushed down about a foot and a half to open the valve of the pipe! There were only eight or nine keys at first, for no one thought of needing more than an octave's compass.

These keys could not be pressed lightly with a finger tip, like those of our modern organ. It took the clenched fist of a strong man to push down the key; consequently an organ-player was called "organ-beater." Later, keys to be played by the feet were added. They were called pedals.

Even when the keys had become smaller and did not have to be depressed nearly so far, playing the organ remained extremely heavy work for a strong man. It was not until a young Englishman, who had studied to be a doctor, set himself the task of overcoming the stiff action of the organ keys that the instrument could be "played" instead of "worked."

In the 1820's a little incident occurred which had a big effect on the life of Charles Spackman Barker, a young medical student of London.

An eminent organ builder, by the name of Bishop, was supervising the installation of a large organ in a neighboring building. Young Barker, passing by, was intrigued by the multitude of pipes—all sizes, from very small to incredibly large—and the great variety of materials used in them. And what a bewildering paraphernalia accompanied the pipes! Keyboards, pedals, bellows, and a great deal of apparatus which Barker could not name. He had had no idea that an organ was such a huge and intricate affair.

Fascinated, the young fellow watched as long as he dared. When he finally hurried on to his studies, it was with only half a mind; the other half remained with the marvelous mechanism of the big organ.

Before many weeks had passed Charles Barker went to his godfather, the generous friend who had taken the place of the parents he had lost in early childhood and was now financing his medical education.

"I'm giving up the study of medicine, sir," Charles announced bluntly.

His godfather stared at him as if he had lost his mind.

"Giving it up! What are you talking about, Charles? You are making satisfactory progress, aren't you?"

"Oh, yes. But I'm not going to be a doctor, after all. I'm going to be an organ-builder."

The older man could scarcely express his incredulity. "Give up a profession for a craft! You can't be serious, my boy. A doctor is respected, revered. It is a career any man could be proud of. But an organ-builder . . . what is he, after all, but a carpenter? This is only a passing fancy, my boy. Keep on with your medical studies. You don't know how lucky you are to be able to get this training."

But young Barker was obstinate. He knew that in organ-building he had found his life's work. In spite of his god-father's opposition, he quit his medical training and placed himself under the best organ-builder he could find (the same Bishop he had watched previously) for instruction.

Two years later, Barker returned to his home town of Bath and established himself there as an organ-builder. Naturally business was slow for a newcomer in the field, and especially for one as young as Charles Barker. But gradually, as time went on, his work became known and respected.

Then in 1832 came a second small incident which had big and unforeseen results.

A new organ had been built in York Minster, a large and very modern one. Out of professional curiosity, Charles Barker went to see it, to determine whether its innovations were worthy of imitation.

He found a large crowd gathered. The new organ had received widespread publicity, and now a concert was being given to show off the instrument's powers.

The organist, one of the best available, made the customary preparations for his recital. He took off not only his coat and waistcoat, but his shirt as well, before he began to play. Yet even in that disrobed state he was dripping with perspiration by the time he had finished his first number. He looked for all the world as if he had been taking part in a violent wrestling match instead of giving a concert!

To Charles Barker this was nothing new. In fact, knowing the organ's mechanism as intimately as he did by now, after several years' experience as a builder, he realized that physical exhaustion was to be expected in even the huskiest organist after a long period of "playing." After all, with several manuals, a pedal clavier, and numerous stops to operate, organ-playing was bound to take on the aspects of a fist fight, with the instrument a tough antagonist. The valve of each pipe had to overcome the pressure of the wind against it before it could open the pallet which permitted the wind to enter. To depress simultaneously several valves required tremendous effort, since the larger the number of pipes called into use at a time, the greater the muscular force required on the keys. The combined resistance was terrific. Barker knew that.

Nevertheless, that day in 1832, at York Minster, he suddenly became aware of the situation as he never had been before. Perhaps it was because this was the largest organ he had ever seen in action, and the organist was endeavoring to bring into play an unheard-of number of pipes. Perhaps it was because the part of the organ which could be seen from the nave of the church was so stately and beautiful, and the performer himself so unprepossessing. At any rate, the contrast between the serene dignity of the organ and its music, and the dishevelled appearance of the organist suddenly struck Barker as incongruous.

Why couldn't something be done to the organ mechanism so that a player could perform on the instrument in suitably dignified attire? No other instrument compelled its performer to discard most of his clothes before appearing in concert; on the contrary, piano, violin, and flute soloists decked themselves out in all their finery for their public appearances. Only the organ exacted such a toll of physical strength that un-dressing, not dressing, was the rule. Wasn't there some way of overcoming the resistance which the keys offered to the fingers?

As he traveled homeward after the concert, Charles Barker found himself obsessed by the idea of reducing the weight of the organ's key action. For days . . . weeks . . . months . . . he thought about it and tried experiment after experiment. But no solution presented itself. Eventually he came to the reluctant conclusion that it was impossible to remove the wind resistance which caused the difficulty of organ-playing. It was simply inevitable that the organist, in depressing a key, should be working against the wind pressure outside the pipe. After all, the voice of the organ depended on that very wind pressure. Remove that and you had no instrument.

Then came the idea: if it was not possible to *remove* the resistance, perhaps there was some way to *overcome* it—maybe by a greater opposing air pressure.

That proved to be the solution. At first Barker used a system of cylinders and pistons, but he soon abandoned that in favor of auxiliary bellows.

He called his device to overcome the stiffness of key action "pneumatic action." It provided each organ key with an air tube which extended to the wind chest. The tube contained air that was *under pressure* when not in use. When the key was pressed, some air was released from the tube into a small bellows. The expansion of this bellows pulled down the pallet or valve of the pipe, cutting down tremendously on the physical force required from the organist's fingers.

Barker knew that he had discovered something momentous in his "pneumatic action." But he did not have the money to promote it. He could not afford to build, himself, organs with pneumatic action. Such organs would be very expensive, since a lever bellows was needed for each key. He must interest wealthy and influential companies in his invention. London was the place to go.

But the organ-builders of London were reluctant to risk money on an untried and expensive innovation. Pneumatic action seemed like a good idea—yes. But it would not be easy to persuade people to pay the extra cost which the apparatus would add to the already high price of a big organ. Moreover, such organs would render obsolete much of their present equipment, as well as the organs they were already building.

At last, in 1837, Charles Barker despaired of interesting his countrymen in his invention, and he went to Paris, where builders were reputed to be more progressive.

He arrived in Paris at an opportune time. The famous organ-builder, Aristide Cavaillé-Coll, was preparing to install a large instrument in the church of St. Denis. Cavaillé-Coll recognized the importance of Barker's invention at once, and incorporated it in his new organ.

The results were all that Barker and his sponsors had hoped for. The wind pressure against the valves, now opposed by the pressure in the lever bellows, ceased to offer stiff resistance to the organist's fingers on the keys. The great organ could be played with as little physical effort as a piano.

One French organ after another adopted the pneumatic action. It revolutionized the whole art of organ-building. There was now no limit to the size of organs or the pressure of wind. Barker soon became recognized as an expert on organs. He built several fine instruments, and later became director of a large organ company in Paris. At the Paris Exhibition of 1855 he received a first class medal and the Cross of the Legion of Honor.

Ten years later Barker made another, and perhaps a greater, contribution to the art of organ building: in collaboration with Dr. Albert Peschard, organist of St. Etienne, in Caen, he devised a way to harness electricity to the organ, operating the pneumatic lever by electricity instead of by air. Now the action of the instrument was truly easy, surpassing that of the piano in lightness. So the electric action enabled the organ to become what it is today, the King of Instruments, and forever took the *work* out of organ-playing. And Charles Spackman Barker proved that he was right to give up the profession of doctor to human beings to become a builder of organs and a doctor to their ills.

19. The Mongrel that Became an Aristocrat

Whether or not you are a pianist, you are familiar with the piano. You have probably lifted the cover of a grand piano, or removed the front panel of an upright, and looked at the array of wires inside. Two hundred and twenty-six strings, if you stopped to count them, ranging from short to long, from thin to heavy, three of nearly every length and thickness.

Perhaps you struck a few keys experimentally and watched

the little felt-covered hammers hit the strings. (The piano, like the celesta, belongs to the percussion family as well as to the keyboard group.) You found that you could play several notes at once, that the tones could be made smooth and legato or sharp and staccato, and that the sound could be as loud and penetrating as a military band's march or as soft and soothing as a mother's lullaby.

Today we take for granted the piano's ability to produce sounds as loud or as soft as we wish, but when the piano was first invented it was that very ability that made it unique among the instruments of its day. And that same faculty was responsible for its original name: "pianoforte" or "soft and loud." The invention probably came about something like this.

In the early 1700's Bartolommeo de Francesco Cristofori was custodian of musical instruments for Prince Ferdinand di Medici in Florence, Italy. It was a position any craftsman might envy: a workshop of his own in the Uffizi, the best tools and materials money could buy, and never a worry about selling the fruits of his labors. Best of all was the appreciation of his skilled craftsmanship that could come only from one who loved music and played it well, like Prince Ferdinand of the Medicis, who was an accomplished harpsichord player.

Yes, it had been well worth-while leaving the shop in Padua where Cristofori had built up a reputation as the best harpsichord maker in the city, to come to Florence to care for the instruments of the most Serene Prince of Tuscany. It was pleasant to work for an employer who appreciated quality; it was inspiring to serve a man who welcomed improvements in musical instruments.

One day Prince Ferdinand sent for Cristofori to make some adjustments in his favorite harpsichord. The instrument maker listened with suitable deference as the wealthy and powerful prince described his objections to the action of the harpsichord.

"Have no fear, Your Grace," Cristofori answered when the prince paused. "I will soon have the instrument as good as new. A few fresh quills are needed, that is all. The quills wear out very fast."

Prince Ferdinand sighed. "Even when it is in perfect condition, the harpsichord does not fully satisfy me. Either it has no expression at all—each note the same as the last—or the contrast is too great if I open the stops, which greatly exaggerates the expression."

Cristofori nodded. Yes, that was the way with harpsichords. No variation of expression, or too much. The clavichord, now, was more responsive. Its tone could be modified by the touch. That was why it was such a favorite with composers for their own private use. But the clavichord's tone was weak. It would never carry in a great hall like this. Hence the harpsichord, with its more powerful tone, was always used in concerts.

"If only," the son of the Medicis was saying wistfully, "If only one could make the tone loud or soft at will. . . ."

The instrument maker looked up thoughtfully. "That would indeed be an improvement. But . . . how could it be done?"

The prince made an impatient gesture. "I don't know. I suppose it can't. I only say I wish it could. Singers can do it.

So can violinists. They can produce any tone shading and any volume they wish. But the poor harpsichord . . . it is sadly deficient in that way."

As Cristofori worked over the delicate mechanism of the beautiful harpsichord, his mind was busy with the question his employer's half-wistful, half-petulant complaint had aroused: how could a harpsichord, whose tones were made by quills plucking its strings, be made to play loud or soft at will?

For many weeks Cristofori mulled over the question as he worked in his shop or on the various instruments in the palace. Whether he was fitting a bridge to a viol, adjusting the tuning pegs of one of the new-fangled violins (probably one that had been made by Stradivarius for the prince), or stretching the strings of a sweet-toned clavichord, the problem nagged at his mind constantly. He began to experiment with harpsichord strings and quills.

Before long he was forced to an unwelcome conclusion: it was simply impossible to vary the tone of a harpsichord appreciably. Every time a certain key was pressed, the quill plectrum stroked the string (much as a harp is played) and made the same sound, equally loud each time. It could not be otherwise. Although the harpsichord had been greatly improved in recent years by the addition of various stops and pedals, individual notes could not be varied.

Cristofori accepted this conclusion unwillingly. It would have been so nice to be able to say to his patron, "I can make for you the harpsichord you have wished for. It will respond to your every desire for loudness or softness." But he could not. He shook his head ruefully and tried to dismiss the matter from his mind.

That was easier said than done, however. Cristofori had solved too many problems of construction in instrument making to admit defeat easily. True, he was certain that the solution of loud-soft did not lie in the harpsichord. But there were other instruments. The large collection of instruments in his custody included many of Belgian, French, and Italian make —even some from Germany. A few were used frequently, others were merely novelties. Cristofori studied them all thoughtfully.

The clavichord, of course, was a favorite everywhere, even though its tone was not strong enough to make it satisfactory for use with an orchestra or a chorus. Its tones were produced, not by plucking, but by brass wedges striking the strings. And the volume could be varied considerably. Perhaps that was the instrument he should work on to satisfy the Prince's wish.

But no. The clavichord was not powerful enough to please His Grace.

Well, there was the old-fashioned dulcimer, from which the clavichord had descended. That little instrument had no keyboard, but was played by hammers held in the hand. Hammers . . . perhaps that was the answer. Hammers attached to keys . . . Hadn't he heard about a fellow named Habenstreit, or something of the sort, who had made an improved dulcimer with keys?

Cristofori began experimenting again.

Before many months had passed he was able to tell Prince Ferdinand that he had almost solved the problem of a loud-and-soft playing instrument. The prince was delighted. He

insisted on visiting the workshop and hearing in detail Cristofori's theories and plans.

Cristofori pointed to a bewildering arrangement of wires,
springs, hammers, and cords. The whole thing looked much
like a Rube Goldberg "Useless Invention" of today.

"The idea is, Your Grace, that when you press a key, a
hammer will strike the string from beneath and drop instantly
back so it will not interfere with the vibration of the string.
Thus, if you want a soft tone, you will press the key easily,
and the hammer will strike gently. If you want a loud tone,
you will press the key forcibly, and the hammer will strike
sharply."

"It sounds simple," marveled his royal visitor. "Why didn't
someone think of it before? But what do all these wires and
things have to do with it?"

Cristofori's face flushed with enthusiasm. "They are the
means of accomplishing this happy result, Your Grace. When
this key is pressed . . . so . . . it acts on this lever . . .
thus . . . which makes this movable tongue force this under-
hammer against the hammer . . . like this . . . which
makes the hammer strike the string above it . . . so. The
tongue is loose, you see, and allows the hammer to fall back
immediately so the string can vibrate; the wire spring brings
the movable tongue back to its original position."

The prince stared at the intricate mechanism. Then he
shook his head. "Such a complicated way of accomplishing a
simple result! This acts on that, which hits the other, which
causes something else to move! It fairly makes my head
whirl."

Cristofori frowned down on his invention. The prince

laughed kindly. "Do not be downhearted, man. I really don't care how complicated the mechanism is, providing it works. Just build me an instrument that can play soft or loud as I wish, and you may use a thousand parts if you like."

But the instrument maker was still frowning. "There are a few things I have not worked out yet. When one wants the sound to cease, the string must stop vibrating. . . . Now, let's see . . . if I attach cloth to a rod which I fasten to the key-shaft . . . then pressing the key would raise the cloth, and releasing the key would allow the cloth to fall and stop the vibrations of the string. . . ."

Prince Ferdinand chuckled. "A few more things in that endless chain of events which you start by pressing a single key! I shall be glad to *play* on your instrument when it is built, Cristofori, but I hope I never have to *understand* it!"

Happy in the approval of his patron, Cristofori spent more and more time on his experimental mechanism. When he was sure his idea would work, he began to build an instrument, using the shell of an old harpsichord.

But he soon discovered that his work had only begun. The frame of neither the harpsichord nor the clavichord was strong enough for the apparatus he had in mind. The cloth-covered hammers he was using, small as they were, had much more force than either harpsichord plectrum or clavichord brass wedge. His strings must be thicker and stretched more tightly. He must have a stronger frame for his new instrument. Not only did he have to devise means of strengthening the frame, but he had to fashion by hand every beam, every plank, every string.

Month after month Cristofori labored, solving one problem

only to find another staring him in the face. But at last his new instrument was finished. It had a compass of 54 notes. The longest string was more than six feet, and the shortest two inches.

It was a mongrel instrument, borrowing features from several sources. From the clavichord it took its striking action and also the practice of tuning two strings to each note; from the harpsichord, its shape (similar to our grand piano); from the dulcimer, its hammers; and, of course, many features came from Cristofori's fertile brain.

Proudly the inventor presented his masterpiece to his patron, calling it *gravecembalo col piano e forte* or "harpsichord with soft and loud."

Prince Ferdinand was immensely pleased. Now he could indeed make each tone as loud or as soft as he wished, merely by the force of touch on the key. The pianoforte became his favorite instrument.

A few years later a writer, Scipioni Maffei, visited Prince Ferdinand in Florence to obtain his patronage for a projected literary work, *Giornale dei Letterati d'Italia*. Maffei saw the new pianofortes and was tremendously impressed with them. He wrote an article about the new instruments and the inventor, and published it in volume V of his book. So the fame of Cristofori's invention spread beyond Florence and all over Italy.

Nevertheless, it was many, many years before the new instrument became really popular. Listeners whose ears were accustomed to the short, thin notes of the harpsichord and the clavichord found the fuller tone of the new instrument unpleasingly robust. Performers found the action very different and hard to master. Only gradually did audiences and musicians become educated to appreciation of the pianoforte.

By that time inventors in other countries had worked out, independently, similar instruments, so that temporarily Cristofori's pioneering work was lost sight of. Today, however, although the piano has been greatly improved by a series of inventions (metal frame, double-escapement, steel wire, etc.) it is generally recognized that Bartolommeo Cristofori, instrument maker to Prince Ferdinand of the Medici family of Florence, was the true father of our modern piano. And the instrument which started out as a mongrel has become one of the world's most aristocratic instruments.

20. Human Keyboard

Do you believe the conductor of an orchestra is a mere figurehead? Do you consider him presumptious to take a bow when you are clapping, not for him, but for the music made by the orchestra?

I used to feel that way, too, until I heard for myself the difference a conductor can make.

It was many years ago, at a convention of some sort. A school orchestra, under the baton of an experienced music supervisor, was playing "The Stars and Stripes Forever." The instruments were all in tune, they played the right notes, they kept together. It was a good student performance. We sat back in our seats and listened. At the end we clapped appreciatively.

Suddenly down the aisle strode a white-haired man in an eye-catching band uniform. John Philip Sousa! "The March King." Composer of the piece the orchestra had just played.

At the supervisor's invitation, Sousa mounted the podium. He spoke a few words, which we in the audience could not hear, to the young musicians. Then he raised his baton. The orchestra came to attention—eager, anticipatory attention.

At Sousa's signal they began again to play "The Stars and Stripes Forever." But what a difference! Same children, same instruments, same notes, almost the same tempo. Yet this time the music brought us to the edges of our seats and set our blood to tingling. At the final note the audience rose spontaneously and clapped and cheered wildly, while the orchestra sat wide-eyed, thrilled and amazed at the way they had been able to play.

Never again could I doubt that conducting is an art. Just as a great violinist can draw more beautiful music from a cheap violin than a poor violinist can evoke from a priceless Stradivarius, so a fine conductor can bring forth better music from a mediocre orchestra than an inadequate conductor can wrest from the finest collection of instrumentalists in the world.

The art of conducting, which has been called the art of talking with the hands, did not spring into being, full-grown, any more than did the modern symphony orchestra. It grew slowly and gradually through the centuries.

For several hundred years the conductor was merely a human metronome: beating time was his only function. Many different ways of indicating the time were used. In ancient Egypt, one of the musicians clapped his hands to beat the time. In ancient Greece, a performer stamped a specially shod foot to mark the beat.

As instruments began to be used in ensembles, the dominant instrument naturally took the lead, and its player automatically became the conductor. Thus the harpsichord-conductor evolved and held sway for about a hundred years. Bach, Haydn, Mozart, and Beethoven (in his early years) conducted from the harpsichord, nodding the head, stamping the feet, or waving the hands when they were not busy on the keys.

As the strings became more and more important in the orchestra, the harpsichord's value lessened accordingly. The violin was now the dominant instrument, so it was natural for the leader of the first violins to take over the direction of the orchestra. The violinist-conductor (called "concertmaster" because he was exactly that: the master of the concert) had several advantages over the harpsichord-conductor: he could stand up, so his cues were more readily visible; he could indicate stress and beat while playing, with his bow and even with his instrument. Sometimes the harpsichord-conductor and the violinist-conductor worked together in the same orchestra; Haydn and Salomon shared the burden of conducting at times.

Regardless of which instrument supplied the conductor, there was no conductor's score as we know it today. Whether he was seated at the harpsichord or standing with a violin, the conductor directed the orchestra from his own part.

Finally, about the beginning of the nineteenth century, conducting by one of the orchestra's instrumentalists declined in favor of conducting by an outsider—an outsider with a baton.

The use of a stick to beat time was nothing new. Off and on for several hundred years, various conductors had used a stick to beat time. As far back as the fifteenth century, choirs were often directed by waving a roll of paper, called a *sol-fa*. Lully had used a stick, a heavy walking cane; but instead of waving it, he had pounded it on the floor to beat the time. His stick finally caused his death, for he hit his own foot with it so hard that the injury resulted in gangrene.

No, the baton was not new in the nineteenth century. But the method of using it was new. It was no longer merely an implement of marking rhythm. It soon became, in expert hands, a magic instrument, soundless in itself, but capable of bringing forth, from a motley collection of fifty or a hundred players, music of incredible beauty.

Along with the baton came the conductor's score. Now that the conductor was no longer tied to a specific instrument, and did not actually have to produce part of the harmony, he was free to look at the music for all the instruments. The music came to be written as it is today: each page contains a line of music as it is to be played by each of the instruments, in the key in which that instrument plays. The conductor must read the page horizontally and perpendicularly *at the same time.* He must not only read it, he must *hear* the music, in advance, in his own mind. And since the music of the transposing instruments (clarinet, horn, trumpet, etc.) is written in different keys from that of the strings, flute, and oboe, the conductor must transpose it as he reads it, in order to hear it properly with his inner ear.

Of all the men who have mastered the use of the slim, simple-looking baton and the complicated conductor's score, none has achieved greater magic with them than a near-sighted cellist who kept a date with destiny in Brazil.

In 1886, nineteen-year-old Arturo Toscanini was almost despondent. After his brilliant record in the Parma Conservatory of Music, the months that had passed since his graduation had been a disappointment. His post as first cellist and assistant chorus-master with an opera company, managed by Claudio Rossi, had not turned out to his liking. The tour of Brazil, which had promised high adventure, had brought nothing so far but irritation and frustration.

Touring itself was bad enough, with the physical discomforts of poor accommodations and strange food. The foreign language heard on all sides was an added aggravation. But worst of all was the atmosphere in the orchestra; quarreling, discontent, open rebellion against the conductor, Leopoldi Miguez. Music—real music—was impossible in such conditions. Toscanini felt he was wasting his time. What was he doing here in Brazil, anyway, so far from his beloved Italy?

When they arrived in Rio de Janiero in June, the company played "Faust" to a full house. But it was not a good performance. The newspaper reviews reviled it in no uncertain terms. Miguez, the conductor, came in for especially severe criticism.

It was the last straw for the harassed conductor. He sent

a letter to the newspapers placing the blame where he felt it belonged: on the singers and the orchestra. He told how he had suffered on this tour discourtesy, ridicule and mutiny from his musicians. And he announced his immediate resignation.

What a predicament! Claudio Rossi, director of the opera company, was half-crazy with shock and worry. The house was almost sold out for the evening performance of "Aïda," and no conductor. The orchestra and the entire company, foreigners all, would no doubt suffer the displeasure of the townspeople, who liked Miguez, a native Brazilian, whether the newspapers did or not.

But the show must go on. It was three hours till curtain time. The assistant conductor, Carlo Superti, was pressed into service. A rehearsal was called; it did not go too badly. Rossi breathed again. The situation could be worse.

When the curtain went up that evening, the manager found that the situation not only could be worse, but *was*. When Superti made his way to the podium, the audience hissed and booed and stamped. Substitute conductor? No! They would have none of him. It was useless, in the pandemonium, for Superti to lift his baton.

Backstage, manager Rossi babbled wildly to himself. What was to be done? The audience was obviously determined not to let Superti conduct the opera. Without a conductor there could be no performance. Without a performance, admissions would have to be refunded. Without gate receipts he could not pay salaries, he could not get another conductor. These unpleasant thoughts chased themselves around his brain in a vicious circle as the uproar out front continued unabated and nervous singers milled around him backstage.

At last Superti gave up, furious and humiliated. Rossi persuaded the chorus master, Aristide Venturi, to try his luck. But the howls and catcalls increased in volume when he mounted the podium. Venturi was no more acceptable to the maddened crowd than Superti.

Backstage, a mob of excited singers and musicians surrounded the frantic Rossi, urging him to action.

"What are you going to *do?*" they asked over and over.

"Do?" the manager sputtered at last in fury and frustration. "What *can* I do? I'm no magician, to pull a new conductor out of a hat."

"Why not try Toscanini?" asked a soprano, on the verge of hysteria.

"Toscanini?" Rossi's voice skated heavenward in incredulity. "He's nothing but a boy—not yet twenty."

"Boy or not, he certainly knows music," a baritone asserted, and a dozen voices agreed.

Rossi closed his ears to the chatter of his unhappy company and the horrible racket that was still going on beyond the curtain. "Without a conductor, no performance. Without a performance . . ."

"Toscanini knows 'Aïda' from start to finish," a member of the chorus affirmed. "Knows how every part should sound. And he never uses a score."

Rossi's mouth dropped open. The manager stared at the singers, listening at last.

"Not only a prodigious memory," another contributed, "but a marvelous ear. Catches every note that's wrong."

It seemed like a slim chance. An audience that had booed

Superti and Venturi was not likely to permit a complete novice—little better than a schoolboy—to conduct the opera. But Rossi was desperate. A slim chance was better than none. He would try Toscanini.

Hastily Arturo Toscanini was summoned. At the unanimous request of the almost hysterical company, he finally agreed to conduct the opera. He started into the pit.

At their first sight of the slight boyish figure in an ill-fitting dress suit, the audience forgot its resentment at being cheated out of the conductor it had paid to see. Perhaps it was sympathy for the young man's nervousness that stilled their tongues. Perhaps it was sheer surprise at seeing another would-be conductor, or amazement that he made no move to open the score on the stand in front of him. Or maybe they were merely getting tired of their noisemaking. Whatever the reason, the audience fell silent, and Arturo Toscanini, for the first time in his life, lifted his baton to a professional orchestra.

At once an electrifying change came over the musicians. From a collection of restless, resentful men, they were fused into a unit. As Toscanini's baton indicated the tempo, their confidence and enthusiasm mounted like magic. At his signal, they began to play. And though each musician had played his score of "Aïda" dozens—perhaps hundreds—of times, this time was different. This time the music was a revelation. Each instrumentalist felt himself important, an important part of a perfect whole, as each key of a piano is essential to the instrument.

It was not only that the tempo was so perfect and so sure; not only that the cues were so clear, the expression so right;

not only that Toscanini's flashing black eyes seemed to each musician to be fixed on himself alone. No, there was more to this young man's conducting than perfect tempo, fine tonal balance, complete familiarity with the score, and sensitive interpretation. There was in him a fire of enthusiasm for the music, a burning ideal of the way the composer meant it to be played. And the orchestra, to a man, caught fire themselves and played as if they were possessed. In effect, the orchestra was a single instrument, on which Toscanini played.

And the audience, which had come to boo the opera company out of the theater, remained to cheer them to the skies.

Thus began Arturo Toscanini's career as a conductor. Because he had the necessary sense of rhythm, keen ear, excellent memory, and solid training in all phases of musicianship, plus the creative imagination of the true artist and the ability to get his vision across to the orchestra, Toscanini was able to keep his date with destiny and turn the opera's failure into success. For the succeeding sixty years he went on from one triumph to another, until his name has become legendary as the paragon of conductors.

Postscript

So much for the *past* of musical instruments. The future is in *your* hands.

Musical instruments have not attained static perfection. Old ones are being changed and improved all the time, new ones are being invented. Perhaps *you* will be the one to develop a reed that will not split, a valve that is impervious to moisture, or a string that neither breaks nor frays. Maybe you, like Sax and Mustel, will invent an instrument that will make a place for itself in the orchestra or band of the future. Who knows?

Bibliography for Musical Instruments

Abele, Hyacinth. *The Violin*. London: W. Reeves, 1938.

Apel, Willi. *Harvard Dictionary of Music*. Cambridge, Mass.: Harvard University Press, 1944.

Audsley, George A. *The Art of Organ Building*. New York: Dodd Mead, 1905.

Bakaleinikoff, Vladimir, and Rosen, Milton. *The Instruments of Band and Orchestra*. New York: Boosey, Hawkes, Belwin, Inc., 1940.

Baker, Theodore. *Biographical Dictionary of Musicians*. Schirmer, 1940.

Barnes, William H. *The Contemporary Organ*. New York: J. Fischer and Brothers, 1930.

Berlioz, Hector. *Treatise on Instrumentation*. New York: E. F. Kalmus, 1948.

———. *Memoirs*. New York: A. A. Knopf, 1932.

Bie, Oscar. *History of the Pianoforte*. New York: E. P. Dutton, 1899.

Blom, Eric. *Everyman's Dictionary of Music*. London: J. M. Dent, 1946.

Boehm, Theobald. *The Flute and Flute-Playing*. Cleveland: D. C. Miller, 1908.

Brinsmead, Edgar. *The History of the Pianoforte*. London: Novello, 1879.

Brown, James Duff and Stratton, Stephen. *British Musical Biography*. Birmingham: S. S. Stratton, 1897.

Carse, Adam. *Musical Wind Instruments*. Macmillan, 1939.

———. *The Orchestra in the Eighteenth Century*. Cambridge, England: W. Heffer and Sons, Ltd., 1940.

———. *The Orchestra from Beethoven to Berlioz*. Cambridge, England: W. Heffer and Sons, Ltd., 1948.

———. *History of Orchestration*. New York: E. P. Dutton, 1925.

———. *The Orchestra*. New York: Chanticleer Press, 1949.

Clappe, Arthur A. *The Wind Band and Its Instruments*. New York: H. Holt and Co., 1911.

Coerne, Louis A. *The Evolution of Modern Orchestration*. New York: The Macmillan Co., 1908.

Daubeny, Ulric. *Orchestral Wind Instruments, Ancient and Modern*. London: W. Reeves, 1920.

Densmore, Frances. *Handbook of the Collection of Musical Instruments in the United States National Museum*. Washington Gov't Printing Office, 1927.

Donington, Robert. *The Instruments of Music*. London: Methuen, 1949.

Ehrlich, David. *The History of the Flute*. New York: D. Ehrlich, 1921.

Elson, Arthur. *The Book of Musical Knowledge*. Boston & New York: Houghton-Mifflin Co., 1915.

———. *Orchestral Instruments and Their Use*. Boston: L. C. Page and Co., 1903.

Engel, Carl. *Musical Instruments*. London: Chapman and Hall, 1875.

———. *Researches into the Early History of the Violin Family*. London: Novello, Ewer and Co., 1883.

Erard, Pierre. *The Harp in its Present Improved State.* London, 1821.

Ewen, David. *The Man with the Baton.* New York: Thomas Y. Crowell Co., 1936.

——. *Dictators of the Baton.* New York: Alliance Book Corp., 1943.

Farmer, Henry G. *The Rise and Development of Military Music.* London: W. Reeves, 1912.

Fetis, Francis J. *Biographe Universelle des Musicians.* Bruxelles: Leroux, 1835.

Fitzgibbon, Henry M. *The Story of the Flute.* New York: Charles Scribner's Sons, 1914.

Fleming, James M. *Old Violins and Their Makers.* London: L. U. Gill, 1883.

——. *Fiddle Fancier's Guide.* London: Haynes, Foucher and Co., 1892.

Flood, William Henry. *The Story of the Harp.* New York: Charles Scribner's Sons, 1905.

Forsyth, Cecil. *Orchestration.* London: Macmillan, 1926.

Galpin, F. W. *A Textbook of European Musical Instruments.* New York: E. P. Dutton, 1937.

Gardner, Carl E. *Modern Method for Drums, Cymbals and Accessories (1945 Edition) Vol. I.* New York: Carl Fischer, 1945.

Geiringer, Karl. *Musical Instruments.* Oxford University Press, 1945.

Giles, Ray. *Here Comes the Band.* London & New York: Harper and Brothers, 1936.

Glover, Ellye H. *How the Piano Came to Be.* Chicago: Browne and Howell Co., 1913.

Goldman, Richard Franko. *The Concert Band*. New York and Toronto: Rinehart and Co., 1946.

Grove, Sir George. *Dictionary of Music*. London: Macmillan, 1904.

Harding, Rosamund E. *The Pianoforte*. Cambridge, England: The University Press, 1933.

Hart, George. *The Violin and Famous Makers and Their Imitators*. London, 1885.

Haweis, Hugh R. *Old Violins and Violin Lore*. London: Reeves.

Hayes, Gerald R. *Musical Instruments and Their Music*. London: Oxford University Press, 1928.

Heron-Allen, Edward. *Violin Making, As It Was and Is*. London: Ward, Locke and Co., Ltd., 1885.

Hill, W. Henry and Arthur F. *Antonio Stradivarius, His Life and Work*. London: W. E. Hill and Sons, 1902.

Hipkins, A. J. *Musical Instruments, Historic, Rare and Unique*. Edinburgh, 1888.

———. *The Pianoforte and Older Keyed Instruments*. London and New York: Novello, Ewer and Co., 1896.

Hughes, Rupert. *Music Lovers' Encyclopedia*. Garden City, N.Y.: Doubleday, Page and Co., 1912.

Kelley, Edgar. *Musical Instruments*. Boston: Oliver Ditson Co., 1925.

Kinsky, Georg and others, editors. *A History of Music in Pictures*. London: Dent, 1930.

Kochnitzky, Leon. *Adolphe Sax and His Saxophone*. New York: Belgian Govt. Information Center, 1949.

Lahee, Henry C. *The Organ and Its Masters*. Boston: L. C. Page and Co. 1903.

Langwill, Lyndesay. *The Bassoon and Double Bassoon.* London: Hinrichsen Edition, Ltd., 1948.

Leeming, Joseph. *It's Easy to Make Music.* New York: F. Watts, 1948.

Mason, Daniel Gregory. *The Art of Music.* New York: National Society of Music, 1916.

Menke, Werner. *History of the Trumpet.* London: W. Reeves, 1934.

Moore, John Weeks. *Complete Encyclopedia of Music.* Boston: O. Ditson and Co., 1880.

Poidras, Henry. *Critical and Documentary Dictionary of Violin Makers.* Rouen: Imprimerie de la Vicomte, 1928.

Posell, Elsa. *This Is an Orchestra.* Boston: Houghton-Mifflin, 1950.

Pratt, Waldo S. *The History of Music.* New York: G. Schirmer, 1907.

————. *New Encyclopedia of Music and Musicians.* New York: Macmillan, 1924.

Riemann, Hugo. *Dictionary of Music.* London: Augener and Co.

Rimbault, Edward F. *The Pianoforte.* London: R. Cocks and Co., 1860.

Rimbault, Edward, and Hopkins. *The Organ.* London: Cooks, 1877.

Rockstro, Richard. *Treatise on the Construction and History of the Flute.* London: Rudall, Carte and Co., 1890.

Sachs, Curt. *The History of Musical Instruments.* New York: W. W. Norton and Co., 1940.

Sandys, William. *The History of the Violin.* London: J. R. Smith, 1864.

Schlessinger, Kathleen. *The Instruments of the Modern Orchestra.* London: W. Reeves, 1910.

———. *A Bibliography of Musical Instruments and Archeology.* London: Reeves, 1912.

Scholes, Percy. *The Oxford Companion to Music.* London & New York: Oxford University Press, 1938–50.

———. *The Mirror of Music.* London: Novello, 1947.

Schwartz, Harry. *The Story of Musical Instruments.* New York: Doubleday, 1938.

Singleton, Esther, *The Orchestra and Its Instruments.* New York: Symphony Society of New York, 1917.

Stoeving, Paul. *The Story of the Violin.* London: Scott.

Straeten, Edmund. *The History of the Violin.* London: Cassell and Co., Ltd., 1933.

Thompson, Oscar. *International Cyclopedia of Music and Musicians.* New York: Dodd, Mead, 1938–49.

Welch, Christopher. *History of the Boehm Flute.* London: Rudall, Carte and Co., 1883.

Widor, Charles M. *The Technique of the Modern Orchestra.* London: J. Williams, Ltd., 1906.

Wier, Albert E. *The Piano.* London and New York: Longmans Green and Co., 1940.

Williams, Charles F. *The Story of the Organ.* New York: Charles Scribners' Sons, 1916.